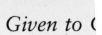 *Given to C*

# Given to God

DAILY READINGS WITH
EVELYN UNDERHILL

*

*Selected and arranged by*
DELROY OBERG

DARTON LONGMAN AND TODD
LONDON

First published in 1992 by
Darton, Longman and Todd Ltd
89 Lillie Road, London sw6 1ud

Introduction © 1992 A. M. Allchin
Arrangement © 1992 Delroy Oberg

ISBN 0-232-51977-3

A catalogue record for this book is available
from the British Library

Cover design by Sharyn Troughton

Photypeset by Intype, London
Printed and bound in Great Britain
at the University Press, Cambridge

# CONTENTS

# ACKNOWLEDGEMENTS

Extracts from *Light of Christ, Collected Papers* and *The Mount of Purification*, all by Evelyn Underhill, are used by permission of the Evelyn Underhill Estate.

Cover photograph of Evelyn Underhill by permission of King's College, London.

This book is dedicated to Terry Snr, Terry Jnr, Tim and Tabitha.

# CHRONOLOGY

1875    Born in Wolverhampton, England, on 6 December.

1888–91 Attended Sandgate House boarding school in Folkestone.

1891    Confirmed.

1897–8  Attended King's College, University of London. Beginning of her period of atheism.

1898    First trip to Italy.

c. 1902–6 Member of Hermetic Society of the Golden Dawn.

1904    Her first novel, *The Grey World*, published.
        First letter from 'M.R.' (Margaret Robinson).
        Beginning of her vocation as a spiritual director.
        Met Ethel Ross Barker, who was to become her best friend.

1907    Conversion experience at Southampton.
        Second novel, *The Lost Word*, published.
        Married Hubert Stuart Moore in July. They lived at Campden Hill Square, Kensington, until 1939, when the war forced them to evacuate.
        Modernist controversy broke.

1909    Third novel, *The Column of Dust*, published.

1911    *Mysticism*.
        *The Path of Eternal Wisdom* (published under the pseudonym of John Cordelier).

1912    *Immanence: A Book of Verses*.
        *The Spiral Way* (published under the pseudonym of John Cordelier).

1913    *The Mystic Way: A Psychological Study in Christian Origins*.

1914    *Practical Mysticism*.

1915    *Mysticism and War*.
        *Theophanies: A Book of Verses*.

1919    *Jacopone da Todi: Poet and Mystic (c 1230–1306)*

1920    *The Essentials of Mysticism and Other Essays*.
        The death of Ethel Ross Barker.
        Conversion to the Anglican Church.

| | |
|---|---|
| 1921 | Baron Friedrich von Hügel became her spiritual director. Delivered the first of the Upton Lectures, becoming the first woman to have her name on the Oxford University list. |
| 1922 | Attended first retreat at Pleshey Retreat House. |
| 1924 | Conducted her first retreat at Pleshey Restreat House. |
| 1925 | The death of Baron von Hügel. *Mystics of the Church.* |
| 1926 | *Concerning the Inner Life.* Bishop Frere became her spiritual director. |
| 1927 | Anglo-Catholic Congress at which she was the only female speaker. Submission for the 1928 Prayer Book. Publication of *Man and the Supernatural* – lectures given at the University of St Andrews, King's College and the Church Congress of 1926. Made a fellow of King's College, London. |
| 1929 | *The House of the Soul.* Became religious editor of *The Spectator*, a position she held until 1932. |
| 1932 | *The Golden Sequence: A Fourfold Study of the Spiritual Life.* Reginald Somerset Ward became her spiritual director. |
| 1933 | *Mixed Pasture: Twelve Essays and Addresses.* |
| 1934 | *The School of Charity: Meditations on the Christian Creed.* |
| 1936 | *Worship.* Gave her last retreat on the Fruits of the Spirit (later published under the same name). |
| 1937 | Publication of *The Spiritual Life*, consisting of the four radio broadcasts given for the BBC in 1936. |
| 1938 | *The Mystery of Sacrifice: A Meditation on the Liturgy.* Awarded an Honorary Doctorate (DD) from the University of Aberdeen, but was too ill to receive it in person. |
| 1939 | *Eucharistic Prayers from the Ancient Liturgies.* *A Meditation on Peace.* *Prayer in Wartime.* *A Service of Prayer for Use in Wartime.* *Spiritual Life in Wartime.* |

| 1940 | *Abba: Meditations on the Lord's Prayer.*<br>*The Church and War.* |
|------|---|
| 1941 | Last ever review published in *Time and Tide*: a review of *Witchcraft* by Charles Williams.<br>Died at Lawn House, Hampstead, on 15 June. She was buried from Christ Church in the graveyard of St John's Parish Church, Hampstead. |
| 1942 | Publication of *The Fruits of the Spirit*. |
| 1943 | Publication of *The Letters of Evelyn Underhill*, edited by Charles Williams. |
| 1944 | Publication of *Light of Christ*. |
| 1946 | Publication of *Collected Papers*. |
| 1948 | *Meditations and Prayers*. |
| 1949 | Publication of *Shrines and Cities of France and Italy*, edited by Lucy Menzies.<br>Publication of *The Mount of Purification*, Evelyn's retreat addresses from 1931. |
| 1954 | Lucy Menzies approached by Longmans Green & Co to write a biography of Evelyn. Lucy Menzies was well into the project when ill health forced her to give it up; she asked Margaret Cropper to complete it. |
| 1958 | Publication of Margaret Cropper's biography of Evelyn Underhill. |
| 1975 | Centenary of Evelyn's birth. A second biography, by Christopher Armstrong, was published as part of the celebrations. |
| 1988 | Publication of *Evelyn Underhill: Modern Guide to the Ancient Quest for the Holy*, a collection of previously unpublished articles, edited by Dana Greene.<br>Publication of *Evelyn Underhill: The Ways of the Spirit*, four of Evelyn's earliest retreats, collected and edited by Grace Brame. |
| 1990 | Publication of Dana Greene's biography, *Evelyn Underhill: Artist of the Infinite Life*. |
| 1991 | Fiftieth anniversary of Evelyn's death. |

# INTRODUCTION

It often happens that well-known writers suffer a period of eclipse after their death. This has certainly been the case with Evelyn Underhill. During her lifetime, and in particular from the publication of her major work *Mysticism* in 1911 until her death in 1941, Evelyn Underhill was one of the best-known spiritual writers in Great Britain. However, after her death her reputation declined. In the 1950s and 1960s she was criticized as someone who had made the spiritual life too comfortable and private, and who had not been sufficiently in touch with the social and political realities of her time. How far these criticisms were justified, readers of this selection from her works will be able to judge for themselves. Such criticisms seem to me to be for the most part superficial and misdirected.

What is beyond question is that in the last ten years interest in Evelyn Underhill's life and work has been growing rapidly, first in the USA and more recently in Britain. It is not too difficult to see why this should be. Evelyn Underhill was a pioneer in the twentieth-century study of mysticism and spirituality. She was a prolific writer who produced many books, some large and academic, others small and easily accessible, but all centred on this one theme. Now, for whatever reason, the last twenty years have seen a great and growing interest in mystical and spiritual questions throughout the English-speaking world and it has been natural for people to turn back to one of the outstanding exponents of these questions from the earlier part of the century.

Evelyn Underhill was also a pioneer in that she was a woman exploring these fields of studies. She was working at a time when it was very unusual for a woman to become an authority on theological matters, to lecture in the University of Oxford, to speak in Canterbury Cathedral, to become well known as a retreat conductor and spiritual director. All these things which would be normal today were not at all normal in the years between the two World Wars, but into all these areas Evelyn Underhill made her way. Quietly and without fuss, she became the first woman to break through into all kinds of realms which for centuries had been exclusively male preserves. She did not indulge in polemic and controversy. She simply went ahead and opened the doors.

Born in 1875, the daughter of a successful London barrister, married in 1907 to a childhood friend who was also a successful practitioner at the bar, Evelyn Underhill's life was outwardly uneventful. She and her husband were in many ways typical upper middle class people of their time. Inwardly, however, beneath the carefully 'ordinary' exterior of her life, Evelyn was anything but ordinary. She was a woman of great intelligence, of great energy and of passionate commitments. For her, as for many of her contemporaries, it was not easy to live a deeply religious life in a world which either ignored religion altogether, or at least took its claims lightly. Her interest in the great mystical writers from the past was far from being simply academic: it was because she longed to live with the same immediacy of contact with the Divine, that she gave so much time to studying and expounding their writings. She longed to make the teachings of the past come alive for her contemporaries and she succeeded in doing this to a remarkable degree. One of the most remarkable qualities of her work, taken as a whole, is the variety of styles which it encompasses, from scholarly editions of mediaeval writers, through essays for theological periodicals, to retreat addresses and meditations intended for lay people of all kinds. In her writing she constantly seeks to combine the analytical with the experiential, the academic with the imaginative in a way which is not at all common amongst theologians and which perhaps reflects a specifically feminine concern for the wholeness of human life and experience.

## Three Aspects of Evelyn Underhill's Teaching

There are three aspects of Evelyn Underhill's life and teaching which seem to me particularly important for us today. Firstly, she knows the vital importance of the inner life for herself and for everyone, the inner life not as 'something specialized or intense . . . not an alternative to my outward practical life but the very source of that quality and purpose which makes my practical life worthwhile'.

She knew from her own experience that to explore this inner life one did not have to be a regular member of any particular Church. For a significant period, from 1907 to 1920, she herself was not a practising member of any denomination. Greatly attracted by Roman Catholicism, there were some aspects of the

claims of Rome which she felt unable to accept. Like the great
French poet of those years, Charles Peguy, she found herself a
kind of excommunicated Catholic. Throughout her life she felt
sympathy with those who find the institutional aspects of the
Christian religion unattractive and repellent. It was only in the
years following 1920 that she finally committed herself to active
membership in the Church in which she has been brought up, the
Church of England. Paradoxically, she became an Anglican at the
very moment when she put herself under the direction of one of
the greatest Roman Catholic lay theologians of our century,
Friedrich von Hügel. She was ecumenical in her very being.

The second point is this. While she knew that the inner life was
a reality open to all women and men, she was profoundly convinced that it was not a private and simply individual affair. As
she says, 'while it requires personal effort and personal choice, it
is also intensely social'. In the realm of our relationship with God,
inward and outward, personal and social meet and interpenetrate.
We are part of a great and living communion of men and women,
a communion which stretches across the centuries and makes light
of the separations brought about by death. Here again she has a
special message for our day. She knows that the words 'the communion of saints' stand not for an abstract doctrine but for a
sharing of life across the barriers of space and time. Tradition is
not something over and done with, a static inheritance from the
past to be contrasted with the needs of the present and the future.
We are rooted in the past not because we are imprisoned in it but
in order that we may be free to grow into the future.

For Evelyn Underhill, tradition means a vital living stream of
experience, of knowledge and of love. She sees the Christian tradition, with which she is most concerned, in all its length and
breadth, Catholic and Protestant, eastern and western. She had a
great love for Italy and for the saints of Italy, especially St Francis,
but she also loved the mediaeval mystics of the Rhineland and of
the Low Countries. The Flemish writer Ruysbroeck was to her the
greatest of them all. She was one of the first to show us the riches
of the English fourteenth century with Julian of Norwich at its
heart. But she also had a deep and vital contact with the Russian
East, with St Sergius and St Seraphim. She would have rejoiced at
the new possibilities of contact with the Orthodox East which are
opening up to us today. Amongst the many tendencies of the
Reformed tradition she seems to have had a special love for

Methodism and for the Society of Friends. All her historical work on the great figures of the past was not done in a spirit of detached historical scholarship; it was done so as to make available to ordinary people something of the riches of our human inheritance, something of the splendour of the testimony of the saints. She opened up, and she still opens up, for English-speaking Christians avenues of exploration which can enlarge and deepen their understanding of the working of the Holy Spirit through the many centuries and cultures which the Church has touched.

But thirdly, all this was not something vague or impractical. She had known, as we have already said, how unattractive the institutional Church can look. But in time she came more and more to see the value of belonging to a particular Church within the whole Christian family. The chapter on the inheritance of the Church of England in her second great book, *Worship*, published in 1936, shows how careful she was to do justice to the different strands which together make up the Anglican tradition as a whole. She herself became a notable exponent of the Anglican way with its respect for tradition and its openness to change, its sense of belonging to a Catholic whole which is more than simply English, yet which has its rootedness in the history and experience of a particular people. She discovered that our commitment to the inner life involves us in outward commitments too. 'When we think of pews of hassocks and the parish magazine we tend to rebel . . . It seems far too stiff and institutional . . . Yet there it is; the Christian sequence is God – Christ – Spirit – Church – Eternal Life.' Every link in the chain is vital. 'The incarnation of the Holy in the world is social.' So it is that Evelyn who for much of her life had avoided making commitments on specific social and political issues found herself at the end of her life, during the first years of the Second World War, impelled to take an uncompromising Christian pacifist stance. She had committed herself to the Church in all its fallibility and limitation. She found herself drawn to commit herself to particular lines of action however unpopular they might be.

### Evelyn Underhill Today

At the Evelyn Underhill festival held in Washington Cathedral early in 1990, one of the most moving and fascinating occasions came on the evening when a number of speakers from different viewpoints spoke of what Evelyn had meant in their own experience. Here was a veteran bishop of the Episcopal Church who had spent much of his life travelling around his far-flung rural diocese, always taking with him a book of Evelyn Underhill to read at the beginning or the end of the day. Here was a distinguished priest of the Russian Orthodox tradition telling us how as a student, like so many others, he had begun to read the work of Evelyn Underhill under the impression that the writer was a man, and how discovering the truth had been for him a first recognition of the importance of the insights of women theologians in the twentieth century. Here was a Roman Catholic laywoman, a person with a key position in the administration of her Church in the United States, telling us how as a young mother with small children she had looked in vain for a writer on spiritual things who was not a priest or a monk or a religious sister; finding in Evelyn a person like herself, immersed in the daily care of her family and the growing demands of professional work, was a liberation for her. I was one of the few people from England at that crowded meeting. It struck me forcibly how mistaken those critics of the 1950s had been when they declared that Evelyn Underhill was a spent force, her writings irremediably marked by the limitations of the Kensington society to which she belonged. It was clear that by their clarity, their intensity, their simplicity and their humour her works had spoken and still speak to people in many different circumstances and many different situations. It is the purpose of this new selection from her books, the work of a student of her writing who lives in Australia, to widen still further the circle of those who can profit from the gifts of love and knowledge which Evelyn Underhill generously offers us.

A. M. ALLCHIN

# SAINTS AND MYSTICS

We are all called to be saints, St Paul tells us (Romans 1:7; 1 Corinthians 1:2), and in more modern times, Karl Rahner has made the startling statement that we must all be mystics too!

Probably most Christians, in all humility, would be reluctant to lay claim to either title. Some may believe they have it all summed up in a way that is the perfect deterrent to aspiring too high: saints are very holy people; mystics are very strange and peculiar. Saints go about doing good works; mystics keep to themselves, are difficult to relate to, and likely to go off into trances, have visions, or levitate during their excessively long hours of prayer. This is far from the concept that Evelyn Underhill would put forward. 'There is no need to be peculiar', she assures us, 'in order to find God.'[1] There is, however, a need to be obedient; and since, at our baptism, we are initiated into a mystical life, we have to face the prospect that God may be calling us to be saints, or mystics, or both – with all that that implies.

The distinction between a 'saint' and a 'mystic' is, in some cases, minimal, and at times Evelyn uses the terms interchangeably and concurrently. 'No deeply religious person is without a touch of mysticism, and no mystic can be other than religious',[2] she wrote.

Yet there is a difference between them, and it is one of degree, of perception, and of experience. The mystic would claim (if forced to admit to it, for real mystics prefer to keep their spiritual state a 'secret') a direct and heightened apprehension of God and a unique and vivid intuition of reality. The mystic 'escapes the sense-world, ascends to the apex of his/her spirit, and enters for a brief period into the more extended life of the All'.[3] The true mystic is a genius in the school of divine love. 'Not to know about, but to Be'[4] is an essential distinguishing element of the mystic's spirituality.

This may go against the egalitarian grain. After all, we are all Christians, and why should some be designated in a special or privileged way, as if they are uniquely favoured by God? But every art and way of life has its specialists, its examples of excellence. As Evelyn points out, we do not 'call everyone a musician who has learnt to play the piano'!⁵ As Jesus warned his followers, 'Many are called, but few are chosen'. It is not that God is unjustly selective and plays favourites. The ones who miss out on the banquet are those who have wives, who have to go and bury parents, who are too afraid to sell everything, or give up whatever is more important in their lives than God. The saints and mystics will not be found among these laggers; they are right up front – not because God allowed them to jump the queue, but because they responded first, and with alacrity, to his call.

The saints, Evelyn describes as 'self-emptied vessels of the Holy',⁶ who have been emptied so that they may be filled by God. What happens after this is what Evelyn calls 'that mysterious give and take between His Spirit and us' in which 'the Divine action comes first'.⁷ This 'given-ness' is, for Evelyn, one of the essential characteristics of true mysticism – or indeed of any spiritual life.

Evelyn writes that there are those who have 'a craving and a capacity for a Reality beyond the bound of sense',⁸ and those people are the mystics. It should be noted that they must also have a huge capacity – if not in this case a craving – for suffering, for the mystic path is difficult, and at times dangerous and frightening. There may indeed be visions, trances, moments of deep ecstasy – but there is also the Dark Night of the Soul to contend with.

Yet both saints and mystics share the same divine vocation: to be tools of the Supernatural, 'Chosen Vessels' of 'the redeeming, transforming, creative love of God'.⁹ They will willingly 'work and suffer in the dark, asking for no assurance of result'.¹⁰ They will, like Jesus, pray from the Cross: 'the arms stretched out to embrace the world, and the eyes lifted up towards the Eternal God.'¹¹

1. Evelyn Underhill, *The House of the Soul*, p. 90.
2. Evelyn Underhill, *Mysticism*, p. 70.
3. *ibid.* p. 74.
4. *ibid.* p. 72.
5. *ibid.* p. 75.
6. Evelyn Underhill, *The School of Charity*, p. 97.
7. Evelyn Underhill, *Man and the Supernatural*, p. 24.
8. *ibid.* pp. 23–4.
9. *ibid.* p. 237.
10. Evelyn Underhill, *Worship*, pp. 167–8.
11. *ibid.* p. 168.

# What is a Saint? (1)

A saint is simply a human being whose soul has ... grown up to its full stature, by full and generous response to its environment, God. He or she has achieved a deeper bigger life than the rest of us, a more wonderful contact with the mysteries of the Universe; a life of infinite possibility, the term of which saints never feel they have reached.

That desire and willingness for growth at all costs, that sense of great unreached possibilities which await the fully-expanded human soul, is important for us all ... If we do not grow thus, the origin of that defect is and can only be in the poverty of our own inner lives of prayer and mortification, keeping that spiritual vitality at a low ebb. Prayer and mortification are hard words; but after all that which they involve is simply communion with God and discipline of self ... All Christians must have in their lives the bracing and humbling influences of such continual self-surrender and self-conquest. They involve a ceaseless gentle discipline; but being a disciple means living a disciplined life, and it is not very likely that you will get other disciples, unless you are one first.

*Concerning the Inner Life*, pp. 15–16

# What is a Saint? (2)

What is a saint? A particular individual completely redeemed from self-occupation; who, because of this, is able to embody and radiate a measure of Eternal Life; whose whole life, personal, social, intellectual, mystical, is lived in supernatural regard. What is a saint for? To help, save, and enlighten by loving actions and contemplations; to oppose in one way or another, by suffering, prayer and work upon heroic levels of love and self-oblation the mysterious downward drag within the world which we call sin. A saint is a tool of the Supernatural, a 'Chosen Vessel' of the redeeming, transforming, creative love of God.

All Saints [i.e. the Feast of All Saints], that glorious, touching Company, will doubtless include many whom the world classes among its irreligious people. Because of 'sin', because of that strange element within the world which opposes God, and perverts His gifts, all such working of the Supernatural in human life must involve suffering and tension. Real temptation, struggle, darkness, is involved in every genuine transcendence of the 'natural man'. Yet since this transcendence is the very condition of the fulfilment of personality, it brings even through effort a real and vivid joy, and ever-deepening peace and harmony, to the soul that undertakes it.

*Man and the Supernatural*, pp. 237, 238

# A Self-Emptied Vessel

The Spirit of Christ is the Church, and the standard of courage, love and self-oblivion the Church asks from each of its members is His standard. Until she gets it her true work cannot be done. We are 'called to be Saints' – self-emptied vessels of the Holy – not for our own sake but for the sake of the world. Every Christian has to look squarely at this ideal. It does not merely mean self-loss in an organized religious society, which depends on God and believes in Him, and teaches morals and faith. It means self-loss in the world's workshop, 'tools of righteousness unto God'; every ounce of energy, all powers and talents, initiative, skill and taste, used – not for us, but for him. When we contrast this programme with our average outlook, it is obvious that real entrance into the Living Church may well be described as a death. For some it is a very peaceful death; but for some a desperate struggle. 'You are *buried* in baptism,' says St Paul to his converts. There is something terrible, a genuine crisis demanding real courage and trust, involved in choosing God.

*The School of Charity*, p. 97

# Real Sainthood: Renunciation

[The saints] know how to take up and turn to the purposes of the Spirit the whole of life as it comes to them from God's Hand. St Bernard and St Francis discard all outward possessions, all the grace and beauty of life, and accept poverty and hardship; and through their renunciation a greater wealth and a more exquisite beauty is given the world. St Catherine of Genoa leaves her ecstasy to get the hospital accounts exactly right; Elizabeth Fry goes to Newgate, Mary Slessor to the jungle, and Elizabeth Leseur accepts a restricted home life; all in the same royal service.

And we see that all these contrasted forms of action are accepted and performed quietly, humbly and steadily; without reflections about the superior quality of other people's opportunities, or the superior attraction of other people's jobs. It is here that we recognize their real character; as various expressions in action of one life, based on one conviction and desire. Thus there is no tendency to snatch another person's work, or dodge dull bits of their own; no cheapening sense of hurry, or nervous anxiety about success. The action of those whose lives are given to the Spirit has in it something of the leisure of Eternity; and because of this, they achieve far more than those whose lives are enslaved by the rush and hurry, the unceasing tick-tick of the world. In the spiritual life it is very important to get our timing right. Otherwise we tend to forget that God, Who is greater than our heart, is greater than our job too. It is only when we have learnt all that this means that we possess the key to the Kingdom of Heaven.

*The Spiritual Life*, pp. 96–8

# The Test of Holiness: Charity and Self-Sacrifice

God is Charity; and the human race has one Lord, who is Incarnate Charity and carries through its utmost demands to the Altar and the Cross. Every decision, therefore, that the Christian takes in life will be controlled by the fact that it must be compatible with following Him. This means that no Christian life will avoid Calvary; though we may come to it by many different ways.

So, because Holiness has entered our world, and appeared in our nature, we know that men and women can become holy; and are bound, in spite of all discouragements, to take an optimistic view of human life. The Church is an undying family which has its face set towards Holiness, and is fed upon the food which can – if we let it – produce Holiness. As the queen bee is produced by being fed from childhood on 'royal jelly,' and thus becomes the parent of new life; so it is what the Christian is given, and what he assimilates of the supernatural food – not what he is by nature – which makes him grow up into the life-giving order of God. The final test of holiness is not seeming very different from other people, but being used to make other people very different; becoming the parent of new life.

It is true that before this happens we must ourselves be changed; must absorb the 'royal jelly,' feed on the Divine Charity. The saints are there to show us that this is a practical necessity, not a devotional day-dream. Their lives disclose to us in all its delicacy and perfection God's creative action in the realm of soul. As we enter into those transformed and sacrificial lives – some of them so near in time and place to our own – we see what it really means to have one Lord. It means everything else in life subordinated to this one fact: no exceptions.

*The School of Charity*, pp. 32–3

# The Test of Sainthood

If we desire a simple test of the quality of our spiritual life, a consideration of the tranquillity, gentleness and strength with which we deal with the circumstances of our outward life will serve us better than anything that is based on the loftiness of our religious notions, or fervour of our religious feelings. It is a test that can be applied anywhere and at any time. Tranquillity, gentleness and strength, carrying us through the changes of weather, the ups and downs of the route, the varied surface of the road; the inequalities of family life, emotional and professional disappointments, the sudden intervention of bad fortune or bad health, the rising and falling of our religious temperature. This is the threefold imprint of the Spirit on the souls surrendered to His great action.

We see that plainly in the Saints; in the quiet steadiness of spirit with which they meet the vicissitudes and sufferings of their lives. They know that these small and changing lives, about which we are often so troubled, are part of a great mystery; the life that is related to God and known by God. They know, that is, that they, and all the other souls they love so much, have their abiding place in Eternity; and there the meaning of everything which they do and bear is understood. So all their action comes from this centre; and whether it is small or great, heroic or very homely, does not matter to them much. It is a tranquil expression of obedience and devotedness.

*The Spiritual Life*, pp. 94–6

# The Threefold Trademark

St John of the Cross says that every quality or virtue which that Spirit really produces in souls has three distinguishing characters – as it were a threefold Trade-mark – Tranquillity, Gentleness, Strength. All our action – and now we are thinking specially of action – must be peaceful, gentle and strong. That suggests, doesn't it, an immense depth, and an invaluable steadiness as the soul's abiding temper; a depth and a steadiness which come from the fact that our small action is now part of the total action of God, whose Spirit, as another saint has said, 'Works always in tranquillity.' Fuss and feverishness, anxiety, intensity, intolerance, instability, pessimism and wobble, and every kind of hurry and worry – these, even on the highest levels, are signs of the self-made and self-acting soul; the spiritual parvenu. The saints are never like that. They share the quiet and noble qualities of the great family to which they belong: the family of the Sons and Daughters of God.

*The Spiritual Life*, pp. 92–4

# Who are the Mystics?

The mystics – to give them their short, familiar name – are men and women who insist that they know for certain the presence and activity of that which they call the Love of God. They are conscious of that Fact which is there for all, and which is the true subject-matter of religion; but of which the average person remains either unconscious or faintly and occasionally aware. They know a spiritual order, penetrating, and everywhere conditioning though transcending the world of sense. They declare to us a Reality most rich and living, which is not a reality of time and space; which is something other than everything we mean by 'nature', and for which no merely pantheistic explanation will suffice. These men and women therefore give precision and an objective to that more or less vague thirst for the Infinite and Unchanging which, even in the rudimentary form in which most of us yet possess it, is surely the most wonderful of all possessions; that sense of another and unearthly scale of values pressing in on them; that strange apprehension of, and craving for, an unchanging Reality utterly distinct from themselves which is the raw material of all religion. And it is through the work done by spiritual genius, its power of revealing to others at least something of that which it finds and feels, that average men and women obtain in the long run all their more vivid convictions in respect of the transcendent world; as through the work done by artistic or scientific genius they learn something of the significance and structure of the physical world.

*Man and the Supernatural*, pp. 21–2

# The Real Mystic

It is a curious fact that those who study and admire the great mystics of Christendom, constantly assume that their experiences belong wholly to the past: that 'modern mystics,' if they exist at all, must be of another species, and express their desire for God in other ways. Yet if the Church be indeed a living and enduring fact, a true organism, the mystical element of her corporate life must also endure, and bring from time to time its gift of supernatural joy and certitude to the common store. Moreover, such a mystical element will retain certain unchanging characteristics, since it arises in the soul's experience of the Unchanging God. Its outward expression may vary: its substance will always be the same. This we have indeed learnt in our survey of the Christian centuries: St Paul joins hands with Henry Martyn, and the period between is filled with men and women who share the same vision, life and power, accept, enrich and carry on the same traditions and speak the same native language of the soul.

It is less easy to show the continuance of this tradition when we come to our own times. Those whose experience is deepest will be least inclined to reveal it, save indirectly, to the world. 'My secret to myself' will always remain true, at least in some degree, of the real mystic; whose contemporaries can only guess at the nature of his hidden life by its results. The fact that certain published works of so-called 'modern mystics' disappoint us by their crude quietism, their shallow volubility, or their un-Christian claim to an exclusive and aristocratic intimacy with God, need not involve the pessimistic belief that the Church can no longer bear and nourish souls capable of a direct and life-giving experience of His richness and love. In every period the number of hidden saints must immensely exceed those whose records are preserved; and even those immediately concerned with spiritual work cannot fully know the amount of genuine mysticism now existing, the numbers of men and women whose lives are centred upon conscious communion with God.

*Mystics of the Church*, pp. 239–40

# A Teacher of the Love of God

When St Catherine of Siena cries 'I have not found myself in Thee, nor Thee in myself, Eternal God!' we recognize a craving and a capacity for a Reality beyond the bounds of sense. If it had not been for the delighted reports and declarations of the mystics and saints, their insistence on its overwhelming actuality, and their heroic self-dedications to that which they have seen, we, little half-animal creatures, could never have guessed that this objective Fact was there, and accessible in its richness and delightfulness to all. Still less could we have supposed that the life of conscious and devoted correspondence with this achieved and all-penetrating Perfection, which is the essence of personal religion, was possible to the human soul.

Those saints and mystics are the great teachers of the loving-kindness and fascination of God. Watching them, we become aware of that mysterious give and take between His Spirit and us by which human personality is transformed and changed: and of the fundamental fact that, in all such give and take, the Divine action comes first. Since we are finite creatures, those ultimate values which convey to us something of the Infinite and Eternal can never be apprehended by our own efforts. They must be given, or infused; and the mystics, and those who know the secrets of contemplative prayer, have been convinced at first-hand of this great truth. God's impact on the soul always seems to them to involve, first, a gift, next a demand, and last the response, gradual growth, and ultimate transfiguration of that soul. This profound sense of something really happening, something done to it and to be done by it, sharply marks off all true religious experience on the one hand from vague spiritual feelings, on the other from those changes in us, and discoveries by men and women which merely develop from within – marks off, in fact, the work of nature from the work of grace.

*Man and the Supernatural*, pp. 23–4

# A Discerner

The mystical type shares in the disabilities which characterize other forms of genius. It discerns more than it can comprehend. It cannot, save by allusion, communicate the substance of its knowledge. We have always to remember the relation in which the most widely open of contemplative minds conceivable by us – anchored, as it must be still, to the conditions of physical life – stands to those realities on which its awestruck gaze is turned; and the drastic process of translation which must be needed before any fragment of its supersensual apprehensions can be imparted to other men. Mystical literature is full of this sense of the over-plus, genuinely perceived by intuition but escaping all the resources of speech. 'Seeing we do not see, understanding we do not understand, penetrating we do not penetrate,' exclaims Richard of St Victor. 'Brother, I blaspheme! I blaspheme!' says Angela of Foligno to her secretary, as she struggles to find words in which to express her great revelations of God. Such genius stretches human awareness to the utmost. It passes beyond 'that encircling wall of Paradise where apparent contradictions coincide', and, because of the strain involved in its special apprehensions, suffers from cruel reactions, distresses and obscurities.

*Man and the Supernatural*, pp. 29–30

# Realist and Transcendent

Only the intuition of the great mystics seems able to know, and give to others in some measure, a spiritual universe and reality which is convincing, all-demanding, utterly satisfying, in its dimly felt and solemn spacelessness, its thrilling attraction and aliveness. This supernal reality these mystics do truly give, or at least suggest to us: not as a possibility of speculation, but as a personally experienced concrete fact, which we are bound to take into account when estimating our sources of information about the world. Thus, as from the great poet we learn the full possibilities and the transcendency of Poetry, it is from the saint that we learn the full possibilities and the transcendency of Religion. We cannot say that he 'understands' it, any more than the brightest and most devoted dog 'understands' canine-human relationships. None the less, incarnated in these special personalities, with their singleness of aim and peculiar sensitiveness, are the racial organs as it were, through which humanity has received the greater part of its fragmentary news about God.

'O Thou Supreme!' exclaims St Augustine. 'Most secret and most present; most beautiful and strong! Constant, and incomprehensible; changeless, yet changing all! . . . What shall I say, my God, my Life, my holy Joy? and what can any man say when he speaks of Thee?'

That is surely the voice of the realist, absorbed in the contemplation of a given objective Fact.

*Man and the Supernatural*, pp. 22–3

# Spiritual Genius (1)

Indeed that which, beyond all else, spiritual genius never fails to give us, is this realistic sense of the overplus of Reality; a perfection exceeding in its totality and splendour all possible human apprehension. What we find is an experience in which personal and impersonal values are combined within a richly living whole. Hence the soul, struggling to convey its apprehension, uses by turns – yet never with complete satisfaction – the language of intimacy, the language of concept, and the language of space. Thus God is felt to be a boundless, all inclusive, all penetrating substance – Ocean, *Patria*, Light. Again He is Life, Joy, Peace; and, equally, a vivid personal Presence – Lover, Father, Friend. We shall not deal fairly with the situation or get any idea of the underlying richness which these stammering and always inadequate terms try to express, unless we bring together all three groups of metaphors; and, keeping ever in mind their allusive and symbolic character, see in them the struggles of the finite mind to suggest its experience of an ineffable Fact.

It is to the writings of the contemplatives, and to the mystical element present in all living theology, that we owe our best conceptions of this richness and distinctness of God; His infinite, spaceless yet vivid personality; the paradoxical union of Unknowable yet intimately known. In the words of Baron von Hügel, the whole outlook of the mystic requires 'belief in a Reality not less but more self-conscious than myself – a Living One Who lives first and lives perfectly, and Who, touching me, the inferior, derivative life, can cause me to live by His aid and for His sake'. All dwell with awe and worship on the contrast between their own state and this holy Reality of God. All have experienced in some measure an Infinite, an Eternal Life, which is no mere unendingness, has in it no quality of succession, but is felt to be 'the All-Inclusive, the Simultaneous, the Perfect, the Utterly-Satisfying'. To say this, is once more to assert givenness: for where, within our poor little temporal experience, could such concepts be discovered by the soul?

*Man and the Supernatural*, pp. 38–9

[15]

# Spiritual Genius (2)

The contemplative is seldom fully conscious of all that this irreducible duality involves; and only in a few rare instances seems able to distinguish, as does Ruysbroeck in a celebrated passage, between 'God and the light in which we see Him.' Yet his or her attitude towards Eternity is essentially and inevitably that of the artist, not of the mathematician; and the contemplative's best declarations and constructions will always have an artistic and approximate character, carrying with them a luminous fringe of significance not amenable to speech. We mistake his or her office if we begin to ask for explanations. Therefore even the report of the greatest contemplative saint is much like that of the wise shepherd; who can tell us much about the weather, but nothing about meteorology, and often supports his rightful judgments by an appeal to imaginary laws. For here, as in all the things that most truly concern our small, emergent, still half-conscious lives, our knowledge, in its luminous and cloudy mass, far exceeds any exact formulation that our science can make of it. Since that knowledge comes to us through a human consciousness – either our own, or that of others – it is, and must be, largely translated into symbols and images, and controlled by the machinery of apperception. In proportion as the spiritual genius abandons first the naïve and then the deliberate use of image and symbol – and he or she is tempted to do this, as their inadequacy becomes clear – so does the spiritual genius abandon the only link between pure intuition (supposing such pure intuition to be possible to us), and our conditioned minds.

Thus when Angela of Foligno says: 'I see all good; and seeing it, the soul . . . delighteth unspeakably therein, yet it beholdeth naught which can be related by the tongue or imagined in the heart. It seeth nothing yet seeth all things, because it beholdeth this Good darkly': she succeeds in producing an atmosphere of ineffability, but actually tells us nothing at all.

*Man and the Supernatural*, pp. 31–2

# Lovers of Reality

The final test of that valid experience of the supernatural which is claimed by the mystics, is never that which they tell us about Reality, but always that which their special experience of Reality causes them to be. It is in their growth, choice, work, sacrifice, endurance – all that they do with the raw stuff of their natural lives, and mostly in defiance of their natural preferences, in and for the felt and loved Reality – that they prove their possession of a spiritual life. That life places the heroic, the unearthly, the absolute, the non-utilitarian love which is fed by prayer, at the very heart of existence; and steadily makes all other interests sub-servient to this. And the result, when seen in its perfect form, is such a complete sublimation of impulse, such a re-direction of life, as makes, in the crisp language of St Paul, a 'new creature' – though a new creature for which, as a matter of fact, most of the old material is cleansed and used again.

It is this transformation, accomplished in its fullness, which makes the saint stand out as a special variety of the race. Indeed, only those persons in whom that costly and genuine change has at least begun to take place, have any real idea of what religion means. The new line of growth thus set going, with its increase in love and creative energy – the real power of the saint to help and redeem others – the social radiation of his or her spiritual force – this seems to result, not from any mere negative sinlessness, but from a certain real though still imperfect sharing in the achieved perfection of Eternal Life.

*Man and the Supernatural*, pp. 46–7

# THE SPIRITUAL LIFE AND
# MYSTICISM

*The main area of differentiation between the spiritual life and mysticism has already been explored in our observations of those who exemplify these states: the saints and the mystics. The spiritual life is a movement, journey, response, growth towards perfect union with God; the 'Mystic Way' is a heightened and intense extension of the spiritual life.*

*Because some of the manifestations of mysticism include bizzare (though to some, enticing) phenomena such as trances, visions, levitations, and other experiences which could be as much symptomatic of mental illness as of spiritual 'genius', it is a dangerous area. Morton Kelsey warns: 'There is a reality of radical evil found in the inner world that is bent on seizing power and destroying the individual . . . The dangers of playing around with the unconscious, with spiritual reality, may be harder to grasp than the tangible danger of playing with an automobile, or with war or atomic energy.'*[1]

*Evelyn Underhill herself exposed certain similarities between mysticism and magic in her book* Mysticism. *She had also been confronted with the possibility of false or induced mysticism in 1908, when she discovered that a number of her non-religious friends were practising a form of meditation (today we would probably call it transcendental meditation) which enabled them to cure headaches and increase their capacity for work. This power to – apparently – get what they wanted by the manipulation of their own psychic states seemed to her to be a 'hypnotic trick' – and she was quite right. Her ability to discern this enabled her to monitor whether or not she was doing the same thing.*

*Until 1920, most of Evelyn's writings involved the use of the term, 'mysticism', and were studies in some aspect of this subject. She had continued to practice a type of mystical prayer, despite the reservations she had had in 1908, and she appeared to have had some experiences which could be called 'mystical'. But she had no objective or impartial assessment of this until 1921, when Baron von Hügel became her spiritual director. The Baron was able to give her assurance that she was not deluded, and provide some criteria by which she could evaluate the experiences herself. His first step of 'de-intellectualizing' her brought home the reality of incarnational, sacramental, and Christocentric religious experience, and supplied what was lacking in her practice of 'pure mysticism'. One subtle revelation of the changes taking place was her preference for the terms, 'spirituality' and 'the spiritual life' rather than the more esoteric and emotive 'mysticism', and this was accompanied by a greater willingness to let God act in her, and to be more receptive to what he was giving. This 'given-ness' was one of the main criteria which von Hügel set down as a proof that a mystical experience was genuine; and in her preface to the 1930 edition of Mysticism, she stated that if she were planning the book again for the first time, she would stress the element of 'given-ness' much more.*

*However, in her own time her approach, and her massive work, were acclaimed, while in our time it has been described as 'the best one-volume study of mysticism', in which is 'grounded a tradition in which mystical scholarship is researched, studied, and interpreted.'[2]*

*One of the strengths and innovative aspects of Evelyn's treatment of the subject is that she endeavoured to adopt a scientific approach to mysticism. Mysticism is 'the science of the Love of God' – in so far as either 'love' or 'God' can be measured! Evelyn certainly did not claim to have fulfilled all the criteria a pure scientist would set down! In Man and the Supernatural she wrote:*

> *We are dealing with human life, the most plastic, most beautifully various and intricate, least standardized of any kind of life known to us. And we are dealing with it, as it acts and exists on that mysterious shore where the physical and metaphysical meet. Therefore we must expect, and indeed welcome, paradox in our efforts to tell at least a tiny bit of what we know of this. We must not demand clarity, consistency, surface logic.[3]*

*From Man and the Supernatural we learn that the type of reality dealt with 'is not a reality of time and space' (p. 22); the knowledge transmitted is frequently conveyed through language and symbol. The language used is personal and impersonal: 'the language of intimacy, the language of concept, and the language of space' (p. 39). The mystics may say much, but effectually tell us nothing!*

The phrase, 'my secret to myself', sums up the rightful reticence with which real mystics regard their spiritual dimension. Their experience will be revealed only indirectly to the world – i.e. through their works.

Here we come to the criteria for evaluating all forms of spirituality. The mystic life 'does not involve an existence withdrawn from common duties into some rapturous religious dreamland.'[4] It is 'social' and 'never self-seeking'.[5] The mystic, like any Christian, has a job to do; Evelyn was writing on 'contemplation in a world of action' long before Thomas Merton. 'Contemplation and action are not opposites, but two independent forms of a life that is one . . .',[6] Evelyn wrote. Mysticism needs embodiment in practical forms and institutions, because it is 'an essential element in full human religion,' but, 'it can never be the whole content of such religion'.[7]

Whether we are using the term 'mysticism' or 'the spiritual life', the criteria comes down to the essential realities of everyday life and language. 'I always have my doubts', Evelyn sensibly reflects, 'about the real sanctity of saints who let the pot boil over or forget to sweep the floor.'[8] The way for each of us is that which will be given and shown by God. Our spiritual (or mystical) lives will consist 'in being drawn, at His pace and in His way, to the place where He wants us to be; not the place we fancied for ourselves.'[9]


1. Morton Kelsey, *The Other Side of Silence*, pp. 71, 73.
2. Harvey Egan, *What Are They Saying About Mysticism?*, p. 40.
3. Evelyn Underhill, *Man and the Supernatural*, p. 41.
4. Evelyn Underhill, *Mystics of the Church*, p. 22.
5. Evelyn Underhill, *Mysticism*, p. 92.
6. Evelyn Underhill, *Practical Mysticism*, p. 156.
7. Evelyn Underhill, *Mysticism*, p. ix.
8. Evelyn Underhill, *The Mount of Purification*, p. 79.
9. Evelyn Underhill, *The Spiritual Life*, p. 34.

# What the Spiritual Life is Not: Specialized and Isolated

My spiritual life is not something specialized and intense; a fenced-off devotional patch rather difficult to cultivate, and needing to be sheltered from the cold winds of the outer world. Nor is it an alternative to my outward, practical life. On the contrary, it is the very source of that quality and purpose which makes my practical life worth while.

Still less does the spiritual life mean a mere cultivation of one's own soul; poking about our interior premises with an electric torch. Even though in its earlier stages it may, and generally does, involve dealing with ourselves, and that in a drastic way, and therefore requires personal effort and personal choice, it is also intensely social; for it is a life that is shared with all other spirits, whether in the body or out of the body, to adopt St Paul's words. You remember how Dante says that directly a soul ceases to say Mine, and says Ours, it makes the transition from the narrow, constricted, individual life to the truly free, truly personal, truly creative spiritual life; in which all are linked together in one single response to the Father of all spirits, God. Here, all interpenetrate, and all, however humble and obscure their lives may seem, can and do affect each other. Every advance made by one is made for all.

*The Spiritual Life*, pp. 24–6

# What the Spiritual Life is Not: Self-Occupied

The spiritual life does not consist in mere individual betterment, or assiduous attention to my own soul, but in a free and unconditional response to that Spirit's pressure and call, whatever the cost may be.

The first question here, then, is not 'What is best for my soul?' nor is it even 'What is most useful to humanity?' But – transcending both these limited aims – what function must this life fulfil in the great and secret economy of God? How directly and fully that principle admits us into the glorious liberty of the children of God; where we move with such ease and suppleness, because the whole is greater than any of its parts and in that whole we have forgotten ourselves.

Indeed, if God is All and His Word to us is All, that must mean that He is the reality and controlling factor of every situation, religious or secular; and that it is only for His glory and creative purpose that it exists. Therefore our favourite distinction between the spiritual life and the practical life is false. We cannot divide them. One affects the other all the time: for we are creatures of sense and of spirit, and must live an amphibious life.

*The Spiritual Life*, pp. 30–2

# What the Spiritual Life is Not: Peculiar!

Extraordinary practices, penances, spiritual efforts, with their corresponding graces, must never be deliberately sought. Some people appear to think that the 'spiritual life' is a peculiar condition mainly supported by cream ices and corrected by powders. But the solid norm of the spiritual life should be like that of the natural life: a matter of porridge, bread and butter, and a cut off the joint. The extremes of joy, discipline, vision, are not in our hands, but in the Hand of God . . . The supernatural can and does seek and find us, in and through our daily experience: the invisible in the visible. There is no need to be peculiar in order to find God. The Magi were taught by the heavens to follow a star; and it brought them, not to a paralysing disclosure of the Transcendent, but to a little Boy on His mother's knee.

*The House of the Soul*, pp. 90, 91

# What the Spiritual Life Means: Give and Take

Spiritual life . . . means the give and take, the willed correspondence of the little human spirit with the Infinite Spirit, here where it is; its feeding upon Him, its growth towards perfect union with Him, its response to His attraction and subtle pressure. That growth and that response may seem to us like a movement, a journey, in which by various unexpected and often unattractive paths, we are drawn almost in spite of ourselves – not as a result of our own over-anxious struggles – to the real end of our being, the place where we are ordained to be: a journey which is more like the inevitable movement of the iron filing to the great magnet that attracts it, than like the long and weary pilgrimage in the teeth of many obstacles from 'this world to that which is to come.' Or it may seem like a growth from the childlike, half-real existence into which we are born into a full reality.

*The Spiritual Life*, pp. 26–7

# What the Spiritual Life Means:
## Being Anchored in God

A spiritual life is simply a life in which all that we do comes from the centre, where we are anchored in God: a life soaked through and through by a sense of His reality and claim, and self-given to the great movement of His will.

Most of our conflicts and difficulties come from trying to deal with the spiritual and practical aspects of our life separately instead of realising them as parts of one whole. If our practical life is centred on our own interests, cluttered up by possessions, distracted by ambitions, passions, wants and worries, beset by a sense of our own rights and importance, or anxieties for our own future, or longings for our own success, we need not expect that our spiritual life will be a contrast to all this. The soul's house is not built on such a convenient plan: there are few sound-proof partitions in it. Only when the conviction – not merely the idea – that the demand of the Spirit, however inconvenient, comes first and is first, rules the whole of it, will those objectionable noises die down which have a way of penetrating into the nicely furnished little oratory, and drowning all the quieter voices by their din.

*The Spiritual Life*, pp. 32–4

# God is All

There is no real occasion for tumult, strain, conflict, anxiety, once we have reached the living conviction that God is All. All takes place within Him. He alone matters, He alone is. Our spiritual life is His affair; because, whatever we may think to the contrary, it is really produced by His steady attraction, and our humble and self-forgetful response to it. It consists in being drawn, at His pace and in His way, to the place where He wants us to be; not the place we fancied for ourselves.

Some people may seem to us to go to God by a moving staircase; where they can assist matters a bit by their own efforts, but much gets done for them and progress does not cease. Some appear to be whisked past us in a lift; whilst we find ourselves on a steep flight of stairs with a bend at the top, so that we cannot see how much farther we have to go. But none of this really matters; what matters is the conviction that all are moving towards God, and, in that journey, accompanied, supported, checked and fed by God.

*The Spiritual Life*, pp. 34–6

# The Secret of Joy

St Paul says that the real sign that God the Giver of Life has been received into our souls will be joy and peace; joy, the spirit of selfless delight; peace, the spirit of tranquil acceptance; the very character of the beatitude of Heaven, given here and *now* in our grubby little souls, provided only that they are loving little souls. If, in spite of all conflicts, weakness, sufferings, sins, we open our door, the spirit is poured out within us and the first mark of its presence is not an increase of energy but joy and peace.

We should not have guessed that. Yet real love always heals fear and neutralizes egotism, and so, as love grows up in us, we shall worry about ourselves less and less, and admire and delight in God and His other children more and more, and this is the secret of joy. We shall no longer strive for our own way but commit ourselves, easily and simply, to God's way, acquiesce in His will, and in so doing find our peace. And bit by bit there grows up in us a quiet but ardent spiritual life, tending to God, adoring God, resting in God.

*The Fruits of the Spirit*, pp. 11, 12

# A Constant Offering

I come now to the many people who, greatly desiring the life of communion with God, find no opportunity for attention to Him in an existence which often lacks privacy, and is conditioned by ceaseless household duties, exacting professional responsibilities or long hours of work. The great spiritual teachers, who are not nearly so aloof from normal life as those who do not read them suppose, have often dealt with this situation; which is not new, though it seems to press with peculiar weight upon ourselves. They all make the same answer: that what is asked of us is not necessarily a great deal of time devoted to what we regard as spiritual things, but the constant offering of our wills to God, so that the practical duties which fill most of our days can become part of His order and be given spiritual worth. So Père Grou, whose writings are among the best and most practical guides to the spiritual life that we possess, says, 'We are always praying, when we are doing our duty and turning it into work for God.' He adds that among the things which we should regard as *spiritual* in this sense are our household or professional work, the social duties of our station, friendly visits, kind actions and small courtesies, and also necessary recreation of body and of mind; so long as we link all these by intention with God and the great movement of His Will.

*The Spiritual Life*, pp. 117–19

# The Hidden Action

We have considered that co-operation with the Spirit's action which is to balance our communion with God, as a giving of ourselves to His service, doing some of His work in the world. But there is another and a deeper side: the hidden action of each soul called by God, the effort and struggle of the interior life – what *we* have to do in response to the Love which is drawing us out of darkness into His great light. Even that mysterious communion with God in which we seek, and offer ourselves to, that which we love – in spite of the deep peace it brings – is not without the pain and tension which must be felt by imperfect human creatures, when they contemplate and stretch towards a beauty and perfection which they cannot reach. Still more when it comes to the deeper action, the more entire self-giving, the secret transformation to which that vision of perfection calls us; and the sacrifice, struggle and effort which, sooner or later, this transformation must involve. The Perfection at which the awakened soul gazes is a magnet, drawing him or her towards itself. It means effort, faithfulness, courage, and sometimes grim encounters if one is to respond to that attraction, and move towards it along the narrow track which leads up and out from the dark valleys of our mind.

*The Spiritual Life*, pp. 98–100

# What is Mysticism? (1)

Mysticism has been defined as 'the science of the Love of God,' and certainly those words describe its essence. But, looking at it as it appears in the Christian Church in all its degrees and forms, I would prefer to call it 'the life which aims at union with God.' These terms – life, aim, union – suggest its active and purposive character; the fact that true Christian mysticism is neither a philosophic theory nor a name for delightful religious sensations, but that it is a life with an aim, and this aim is nothing less than the union of the spirit with the very Heart of the Universe.

That more or less vivid experience of God which may come early in the mystic's career, and always awakens a love and a longing for Him, is, so to speak, only the raw material of real mysticism. It is in the life and growth which follow upon this first apprehension, the power developed, the creative work performed, that we discover its true value and its place in the economy of the spiritual world.

*Mystics of the Church*, pp. 21, 22

# What is Mysticism? (2)

By Christian mysticism we mean a conscious growing life of a special kind: that growth in 'love, true Being, and creative spiritual Personality' which has been described as the essence of holiness. This life does not involve an existence withdrawn from common duties into some rapturous religious dreamland, which many people suppose to be mystical. The hard and devoted life of some of the greatest mystics of the Church at once contradicts this view. It is a life inspired by a vivid and definite aim; the life of a dedicated will moving steadily in one direction, towards a perfect and unbroken union with God. Whatever form the experience of the mystics took – whether expressed in the deep peace of contemplative prayer or in ecstasy and other 'abnormal ways' – at bottom all comes down to this. They felt, or rather feel – for there are plenty of them in the world today – an increasing and overwhelming certainty of first-hand contact with God, penetrating and transfiguring them. By it they were at once deeply humbled yet intensely stimulated: it became, once for all, the supreme factor in their lives, calling forth a total response from mind, feeling and will.

*Mystics of the Church*, p. 22

# What is Mysticism? (3)

People talk about mysticism as if it were something quite separate from practical religion; whereas, as a matter of fact, it is the intense heart of all practical religion, and no one without some touch of it is contagious and able to win souls. What *is* mysticism? It is in its widest sense the reaching out of the soul to contact with those eternal realities which are the subject matter of religion. And the mystical life is the complete life of love and prayer which transmutes those objects of belief into living realities: love and prayer directed to God for Himself, and not for any gain for ourselves.

All our external religious activities – services, communions, formal devotions, good works – these are either the expressions or the support of this inward life of loving adherence. We must have such outward expressions and supports, because we are not pure spirits but human beings, receiving through our senses the messages of Reality. But all their beauty is from within; and the degree in which we can either exhibit or apprehend that beauty depends on our own inward state. I think that if this were more fully realized, a great deal of the hostility which is now shown to institutional religion by good and earnest people would break down.

*Concerning the Inner Life*, pp. 17–18

# Practical Mysticism

The mystical consciousness has the power of lifting those who possess it to a plane of reality which no struggle, no cruelty, can disturb: of conferring a certitude which no catastrophe can wreck. Yet it does not wrap its initiates in a selfish and other-worldly calm, isolate them from the pain and effort of the common life. Rather it gives them renewed vitality; administering to the human spirit not – as some people suppose – a soothing draught, but the most powerful of stimulants. Stayed upon eternal realities, that spirit will be far better able to endure and profit by the stern discipline which the race is now called to undergo [World War I], than those who are wholly at the mercy of events; better able to discern the real from the illusory issues, and to pronounce judgment on the new problems, new difficulties, new fields of activity now disclosed.

No nation is truly victorious which does not emerge with its soul unstained. If this be so, it becomes a part of true patriotism to keep the spiritual life, both of the individual citizen and of the social group, active and vigorous; its vision of realities unsullied by the entangled interests and passions of the time. The spiritual life is not a special career, involving abstraction from the world of things. It is a part of everyone's life; and until we have realised it we are not complete human beings, have not entered into possession of all our powers. It is therefore the function of a practical mysticism to increase, not diminish, the total efficiency, the wisdom and steadfastness, of those who try to practice it.

*Practical Mysticism*, pp. ix–xi

# The Need for Mystics

It is certain that the Christian Church has never been without mystics; that is to say, persons capable of direct experience of God and of spiritual things. Yet there are periods in which this mystical instinct seems to rise to the surface of her conscious life, expressed in some great personality or group of personalities. Then it becomes articulate, and starts a fresh current of thought and feeling in respect of the infinite mysteries of God.

Any short account of the mystics of the Church must fix our attention on these landmarks. But their significance is only understood if we remember that they are not solitary beacons set up in the arid wilderness of 'external religion'; they are rather surviving records of a spiritual culture, content, for the most part, to live in secret, and leaving few memorials behind. The stretches of country between them were inhabited by countless humble spirits, capable in their own degree of first-hand experience of God. Only realizing this can we reach a true conception of the perennial richness and freshness of the Church's inner life.

Thus, the importance of St Paul's epistles does not abide only in their writer's mystical greatness, his unique power of describing the mysterious intercourse of the Christian soul with Christ, but also, indeed largely, in the fact that the persons St Paul was addressing included some capable of understanding the height, breadth and depth of his utterance; of sharing his vision and joy. This means that in the Primitive Church St Paul's experience was not unique in kind, but only in degree. So, too, the significance of Cassian's *Dialogues*, or of the literature produced in the fourteenth century by the Friends of God, lies in the fact that they do not merely tell the experiences of one privileged spirit; but represent and minister to the mystical demands of a whole period eager for, and able to assimilate, the secrets of the contemplative life.

Mysticism only thus becomes articulate when there is a public which craves for the mystic's message; for except in response to the need of others, it is the instinct of all contemplatives to keep their secret to themselves.

*Mystics of the Church*, pp. 53–4

[ 34 ]

# The Mystic Way

A discussion of mysticism, regarded as a form of human life, will include two branches. First the life process of the mystic: the remaking of personality; the method by which his or her peculiar consciousness of the Absolute is attained, and faculties which have been evolved to meet the requirements of the phenomenal, are enabled to do work on the transcendental, plane. This is the 'Mystic Way' in which the self passes through the states or stages of development which were codified by the Neoplatonists, and after them by the mediaeval mystics, as Purgation, Illumination, and Ecstasy. Secondly, the content of the mystical field of perception; the revelation under which the contemplative becomes aware of the Absolute. This will include a consideration of the so-called doctrines of mysticism: the attempts of the articulate mystic to sketch for us the world into which he or she has looked, in language which is only adequate to the world in which the rest of us dwell. Here the difficult question of symbolism, and of symbolic theology, comes in: a point upon which many promising expositions of the mystics have been wrecked. It will be our business to strip off as far as may be the symbolic wrapping, and attempt a synthesis of these doctrines; to resolve the apparent contradictions of objective and subjective revelations, of the ways of negation and affirmation, emanation and immanence, surrender and deification, the Divine Dark and the Inward Light; and finally to exhibit, if we can, the essential unity of that experience in which the human soul enters consciously into the Presence of God.

*Mysticism*, p. 94

# True Mysticism

*True Mysticism is never self-seeking.* It is not, as many think, the pursuit of supernatural joys; the satisfaction of a high ambition. The mystics do not enter on the quest because they desire the happiness of the Beatific Vision, the ecstasy of union with the Absolute, or any other personal reward. That noblest of all passions, the passion for perfection for Love's sake, far outweighs the desire for transcendental satisfaction. 'O Love,' said St Catherine of Genoa, 'I do not wish to follow thee for sake of these delights, but solely from the motive of true love.' Those who do otherwise are only, in the plain words of St John of the Cross, 'spiritual gluttons', or, in the milder metaphor here adopted, magicians of the more high-minded sort. The true mystics claim no promises and make no demands. They go because they must, as Galahad went towards the Grail: knowing that for those who can live it, this alone is life. They never rest in that search for God which they hold to be the fulfilment of their highest duty; yet they seek without any certainty of success.

Like their type, the 'devout lover' of romance, then, the mystics serve without hope of reward. By one of the many paradoxes of the spiritual life, they obtain satisfaction because they do not seek it; complete their personality because they give it up. 'Attainment,' says Dionysius the Areopagite in words which are writ large on the annals of Christian ecstasy, 'comes only by means of this sincere, spontaneous, and entire surrender of yourself and all things.' Only with the annihilation of selfhood comes the fulfilment of love. Were the mystics asked the cause of their often extraordinary behaviour, their austere and steadfast quest, it is unlikely that their reply would contain any reference to sublime illumination or unspeakable delights. It is more probable that they would answer in some such words as those of Jacob Boehme, 'I am not come to this meaning, or to this work and knowledge through my own reason or through my own will and purpose; neither have I sought this knowledge, nor so much as to know anything concerning it. I sought only for the heart of God, therein to hide myself.'

*Mysticism*, pp. 92–3

# Realism and Illusion

'Whether we live or whether we die,' said St Paul, 'we are the Lord's.' The mystic is a realist, to whom these words convey not a dogma but an invitation: an invitation to the soul to attain that fullness of life for which she was made, to 'lose herself in That which can be neither seen nor touched; giving herself entirely to this sovereign Object without belonging either to herself or to others: united to the Unknown by the most noble part of herself and because of her renouncement of knowledge; finally drawing from this absolute ignorance a knowledge which the understanding knows not how to attain.' Mysticism, then, is seen as the 'one way out' for the awakened spirit; healing that human incompleteness which is the origin of our divine unrest. 'I am sure,' says Eckhart, 'that if a soul knew the very least of all that Being means, it would never turn away from it.' The mystics have never turned away: to do so would have seemed to them a self-destructive act. Here, in this world of illusion, they say, we have no continuing city. This statement, to you a proposition, is to us the central fact of life. 'Therefore, it is necessary to hasten our departure from hence, and detach ourselves in so far as we may from the body to which we are fettered, in order that with the whole of our selves, we may fold ourselves about Divinity, and have no part void of contact with Him.'

*Mysticism*, p. 93

# The Spiritual Spark

To sum up. Mysticism is seen to be a highly specialized form of that search for reality, for heightened and completed life, which we have found to be a constant characteristic of human consciousness. It is largely prosecuted by that 'spiritual spark,' that transcendental faculty which, though the life of our life, remains below the threshold in ordinary people. Emerging from its hiddenness in the mystic, it gradually becomes the dominant factor in his life; subduing to its service, and enhancing by its saving contact with reality, those vital powers of love and will which we attribute to the heart, rather than those of mere reason and perception, which we attribute to the head. Under the spur of this love and will, the whole personality rises in the acts of contemplation and ecstasy to a level of consciousness at which it becomes aware of a new field of perception. By this awareness, by this 'loving sight,' it is stimulated to a new life in accordance with the Reality which it has beheld. So strange and exalted is this life, that it never fails to provoke either the anger or the admiration of others. 'If the great Christian mystics,' says Leuba, 'could by some miracle be all brought together in the same place, each in his habitual environment, there to live according to his manner, the world would soon perceive that they constitute one of the most amazing and profound variations of which the human race has yet been witness.'

*Mysticism*, pp. 93–4

# THE CHURCH

Evelyn Underhill was baptized and confirmed in the Anglican Church at the age when such sacraments were formally administered, and she probably had as much conviction and commitment as the majority who soon fell away. By the time she was seventeen, Evelyn, like her parents, had ceased regular Church attendance, regarding the institution merely as a facility for weddings and funerals, and for the provision of pompous ceremonies on public occasions.

However, her travels in Italy and on the continent from 1898 onwards, and especially the time she spent visiting the famous churches and shrines, sowed the seeds of a deep and enduring respect and fascination for the Roman Catholic religion. Back in England she cultivated this seed, attending Mass in Roman Catholic churches, as well as some services in her 'own' Church. Thus began her spiritual journey which, after a dramatic conversion experience in February 1907, appeared to be leading her towards Roman Catholicism.

This, however, was not to be. There were personal reasons – her fiancé refused to marry her if she converted; and intellectual – the Modernist 'heresy' provoked much bitter controversy in the Roman Catholic Church and resulted in fierce and unjust persecution of people like Tyrrell, whom Evelyn admired greatly. Evelyn considered herself a Modernist on many points, and experienced her first disillusionment with the Church she had hoped to make her own.'The narrow exclusiveness of Rome is dreadful', she declared. 'I could never believe it, for I feel in sympathy with Christians of every sort – except when they start hating one another.'[1] Sympathy, however, was not allegiance, and to join any other communion, especially Anglicanism, was 'simply an impossible thought'.[2]

Her early experiences of the Church of England had indeed left her unimpressed and repelled. Perhaps she had just been unlucky. Lucy Menzies, in her unpublished biography of Evelyn, observed:

Her foreign travels had shown her the Church of Rome at its

*best: so far she had never seen the Church of England at its best.*

Even at its best, and after she had been a communicating member for many years, Evelyn still saw the Church of England as merely 'a respectable suburb of the city of God – but all the same, part of "Greater London" '[3] or as a 'Bridge Church'.[4]

But once 'in', she did not look back:

> ... our Lord has put me here, keeps on giving me more and more jobs to do for souls here ... I am meant to stay here and not 'down tools' ... After all He has lots of terribly hungry sheep in Wimbledon, and if it's my job to try and help with them a bit it is no use saying I should rather fancy a flat in Mayfair, is it?[5]

Her commitment to this vocation bore much fruit. Margaret Cropper points out that 'she not only found her own nesting place in the C. of E. but showed many others the way there.'[6]

The Church to which she introduced these others was far from flawless. Evelyn greatly admired the influence which the Oxford reformers had had on the Church of England; but what she saw in many Churches did not reflect their ideals at all. She was critical of 'the dreary character of many Church services', and clergy who were lax in their clerical duties and the cultivation of their interior lives. Probably she could not have survived in this atmosphere of apathy had she not had a tremendous sense of humour and a right sense of priorities: God and the great centralities of religion first, and not 'the Vicar and the curate and the Mothers' Union Committee'.[7]

Evelyn applied the criterion of Newman – who, as we know, did leave the Anglican Church and convert to Roman Catholicism. He stated that, 'to breed saints is the proper task of the visible Church.'[8] In a paper to the Newcastle Theological Society, Evelyn affirmed her belief that the final test of any religious movement, 'is not to be sought in the realm of doctrine and practice but in the souls that it forms'.[9]

She does not mean this to sound like spiritual self-indulgence and self-absorption. She continually reminds us that both the Church and its worship have a social character, and that this includes the living as well as those who have died. Though corporate worship is a means of being 'fed' and should have 'a steadying and mellowing effect'[10] which will carry us over the rough patches, we are obliged in our turn to share this food with our neighbours in loving Christian service.

In reality, we know that the Church constantly fails us and itself, and thus fails God. The modern Church is regularly rocked with scandals and heresies, hampered by apathy and cynicism, and shamed by its own lack of conviction in what it should witness to: God, and the priority of God.

The Church Evelyn holds up to us in these extracts is often the ideal. It is not the Church with which many worshippers would readily identify. But it is the Church we should want to have, and want to be part of. And if it is not, we must look to ourselves, and to the quality of our witness.

> As a member of the Mystical Body of Christ, a unit of the Church, I must in some way show these states and characteristics of Christ in my life, some more, some less, according to my special call. I am part of the organism through which Christ continues to live in the world. I too am required to incarnate something of His all-generous and redeeming spirit, share my knowledge of Him, give myself without stint to heal and save other children of God at my own cost. How does my life stand that test?'[11]

1. Charles Williams (ed.), *The Letters of Evelyn Underhill*, p. 126.
2. *ibid*. p. 126.
3. *ibid*. p. 195.
4. *ibid*. p. 275.
5. *ibid*. pp. 195–6.
6. Margaret Cropper, *Evelyn Underhill*, p. 63.
7. Charles Williams, *op. cit.*, pp. 207–8.
8. Evelyn Underhill, *Worship*, p. 330.
9. Margaret Cropper, *Evelyn Underhill*, p. 176.
10. Charles Williams, *op. cit.*, p. 312.
11. Evelyn Underhill, *Light of Christ*, p. 33.

# What is the Church?

'I believe One Catholic and Apostolic Church.' We must believe someone. We believe, then, the united voice of Christendom; its statements about Reality, as given in its Scriptures, its Liturgy, its Sacraments, and by its Saints. We make its Creeds, its solemn pronouncements regarding the essentials of Faith, our standard, trust them, take them seriously: not as a particular way of dealing with life – something that happens to appeal to us – but as *the* way of dealing with life. Though the architecture be old-fashioned and the lighting defective, here God in His humility tabernacles among us.

So, because we believe in that holy and life-giving Spirit who becomes articulate in the prophets, telling us their vision of God, we also believe, which is often far more difficult, the voice of the traditional Church. When that voice has a horribly official accent, or makes to our minds impossibly concrete statements, we acknowledge that it is possibly our stupidity and not her stuffiness which makes our sympathy so incomplete. She does offer to us – and not to us alone, but to everyone who will listen – the supernatural poetry and the supernatural music on a wave-length we can receive. She witnesses within the world to the Fact of God. All her symbolic veils do give us something of the radiance of the uncreated Light, and within her ancient phrases we hear the murmur of the one Word. And more than this, we acknowledge that the total Christian society, the 'Company of Faithful People' – even as we experience it here, in the unfortunate form of a club which is far too full of mutually exclusive *cliques* – has yet a quality, a personality, a power of its own. Its baptism, the mutual act in which we enter its ranks and it cleanses and receives us, does something; knocks off the fetters of our sub-human past, admits us to a new level of life, makes us the citizens of another Patria, with a real and awful series of privileges and powers and a real and awful series of responsibilities.

*The School of Charity*, pp. 90–2

# What the Church Is – and Is Not!

In the world of spirit, that which is done by one is done for all, since the real actor is always the Charity of God. The inner lives of Christians, however deeply hidden, are never private. So far as those lives are real, the Spirit who indwells the Church prays and adores in *them*, strives in *them* and reaches out through *them*. Therefore, because of the Church, when we pray we pray with all the Saints: in whom this is happening too. Thus the radiation of the humblest prayer affects the whole Body's life, and when we fail to do our part its whole spiritual effectiveness is correspondingly diminished. We are added to the Church, as Cardinal Mercier said, not merely for the sake of our own souls, but 'in order to extend the Kingdom of Love.'

For the reality of the Church does not abide in us; it is not a spiritual Rotary Club. Its reality abides in the One God, the ever-living One whose triune Spirit fills it by filling each one of its members. We build up the Church best, not by a mere overhaul of the fabric and the furniture, desirable as this may sometimes be, but by opening ourselves more and more with an entire and humble generosity to that Spirit-God Who is among us as one that serveth, and reaches out through His Church towards all souls. Thus the real life of that Church consists in the mutual love and dependence, the common prayer, adoration and self-offering of the whole inter-penetrating family of spirits who have dared to open their souls without condition to that all-demanding and all-giving Spirit of Charity, in Whom we live and move and without Whom we should not exist.

*The School of Charity*, pp. 99–100

# The Purpose of the Church

The Church is in the world to save the world. It is a tool of God for that purpose; not a comfortable religious club established in fine historical premises. Every one of its members is required, in one way or another, to co-operate with the Spirit in working for that great end: and much of this work will be done in secret and invisible ways. We are transmitters as well as receivers. Our contemplation and our action, our humble self-opening to God, keeping ourselves sensitive to His music and light, and our generous self-opening to our fellow creatures, keeping ourselves sensitive to their needs, ought to form one life; meditating between God and His world, and bringing the saving power of the Eternal into time. We are far from realizing all that human spirits can do for one another on spiritual levels if they will pay the price; how truly and really our souls interpenetrate, and how impossible and un-Christian it is to 'keep ourselves to ourselves.' When St Catherine of Siena used to say to the sinners who came to her: 'Have no fear, I will take the burden of your sins,' she made a practical promise, which she fulfilled literally and at her own great cost. She could do this because she was totally self-given to the purposes of the Spirit, was possessed by the Divine passion of saving love, and so had taken her place in the great army of rescuing souls.

*The Spiritual Life*, pp. 88–9

# The Communion of Saints

A real Church has something to give to, and something to demand from each of its members, and there is a genuine loss for anyone in being unchurched. Because it endures through a perpetual process of discarding and renewal, those members will share the richness and experience of a spiritual life far exceeding their own time-span; a truth which is enshrined in the beautiful conception of the Communion of Saints. They enter a group-consciousness which reinforces their own in the extent to which they surrender to it; which surrounds them with favourable suggestions and gives the precision of habit to their instinct for Eternity. The special atmosphere, the hoarded beauty, the evocative yet often archaic symbolism of a Gothic Cathedral, with its constant reminiscences of past civilizations and old levels of culture, its broken fragments and abandoned altars, its conservation of eternal truths – the intimate union in it of the sublime and homely, the successive and abiding aspects of reality – make it the most fitting of all images of the Church, regarded as the spiritual institution of humanity. And the perhaps undue conservatism commonly associated with Cathedral circles represents too the chief reproach which can be brought against churches – their tendency to preserve stability at the expense of novelty, to crystallize, to cling to habits and customs which no longer serve a useful end. In this a church is like a home; where old bits of furniture have a way of hanging on, and old habits, sometimes absurd, endure. Yet both the home and the church can give something which is nowhere else obtainable by us, and represent values which it is perilous to ignore. When once the historical character of reality is fully grasped by us, we see that some such organization through which achieved values are conserved and carried forward, useful habits are learned and practised, the direct intuitions of genius, the prophet's revelation of reality are interpreted and handed on, is essential to the spiritual continuity of the race: and that definite churchmanship of some sort, or its equivalent, must be a factor in the spiritual reconstruction of society.

*The Life of the Spirit and The Life of Today*, pp. 128–9

[ 45 ]

# The Body of Christ

If we believe in the Church as a living spiritual reality, we must act in harmony with that belief, as members of the Church. This means much more than doing our bit in the matter of corporate worship; though it will certainly include that expression of our social obligations. It will mean, says St Paul, 'becoming obedient from the heart' – the very core of personality – 'to that form of teaching whereunto ye were delivered.' That is a demand for the complete transformation of life. It means that being Members of the Body of Christ is to be the ruling fact about us. Crossing over to the divine side with all our powers, we must take a humble place in the ranks: become part of the reasonable, holy and living sacrifice. It means that in work and prayer, suffering and self-conquest, we are never to forget that we do not act alone or for ourselves. We act with and for the whole body. The prayer of the individual Christian is always the prayer of the whole Church; and therefore it is infinite in its scope.

In his letter to the Romans, we find St Paul asking his converts if they realize what it means to be part of the Church. It means, he says, being received into the death of Christ – the unconditional sacrifice of the Cross – in order to walk in newness of life: transformed through self-loss into a bit of that Body which is indwelt and ruled by the Spirit of Divine Charity. No easy application for membership, then, fulfils the demands of real Christianity. It is a crisis, a radical choice, a deep and costly change. When we judge our own lives by this standard we realize that full entrance into the Church's real life must for most of us be a matter of growth. There are many things the Spirit could do through us, for the healing and redeeming of the world, if it were not for our cowardice, slackness, fastidiousness, or self-centred concentration on our own jobs. Individual Christians cannot attain their full stature till they throw in their hand with the saints and the angels: more, with the broken, the struggling and the meek. But most of us are too prudent, too careful to do that.

*The School of Charity*, pp. 94–6

# The Divine Society

As, then, we believe in the Holy Spirit – Divine Love, issuing eternally from the Heart of God – we believe also in the Church, the Divine Society, the matrix which receives and gives expression to that love; and we acknowledge that by entering this Society our whole situation is changed. We become by this act part of a Body, a Communion, in which the Spirit is perpetually re-born in poverty and hardness; and perpetually continues in and through its Saints – here in one way, there in another – its ceaseless oblation of love. A body in which every living cell is, as St John Eudes boldly insisted, 'part of Christ Himself'; part of the redeeming life at work within the world. Part, therefore, of a life which may be called to endure betrayal, mockery, crucifixion, darkness and apparent defeat, and give new life through this apparent defeat.

This means that the sufferings of the Body, all its divisions, struggles, persecutions, imperfections, deeply concern every member, and that the mysterious sacrificial action of the Body, which embraces, sweetens and sanctifies all its activities and turns them into love, must also be the secret action of each soul.

*The School of Charity*, p. 98

# The Pattern of Perfection

When the Christians looks at the Crucifix, they look at that which is for them the Pattern of all perfection; the double revelation of God's love towards them and their love towards God, the heart of Charity. But they are also looking at the Church, that real Church which is a holy and living Sacrifice eternally self-offered to God; the Body of Christ, the number of whose members no one knows but God alone, and which is the living instrument of His creative love within this world. 'Wherever Christ is,' said St Ignatius of Antioch, 'there is the Catholic Church.' So, to be a member of the Church means not merely conformity to an institution, but incorporation in that living organism which only exists to express the Thought of God. It means becoming part of that perpetual sacrifice which continues in space and time the life of Incarnate Charity. In the name of all her members, the Church comes up to the altar with awe and thanksgiving, and there, on the very frontiers of the unseen world, she gives herself that she may receive the Food of Eternal Life. So the inner life of each one of those members must have in it the colour of sacrifice, the energy of a redeeming love, if it is to form part of the living Soul of the Church. The unceasing liturgic life of the official Church, her prayer and adoration, her oblation and communion, only has meaning as the expression of that soul: the voice of the Communion of Saints. But as this, it has a meaning, a splendour and a claim on us, far transcending those private prayers to which we are apt to give priority. The whole poetry of our relation to the unseen Love is hidden in the Liturgy: with its roots in history, its eyes set upon Eternity, its mingled outbursts of praise and supplication, penitence and delight, it encloses and carries forward the devotion of the individual soul, lost in that mighty melody. To say, then, that we believe the corporate voice of those who make this melody, whose separate lives are lost in it and who are our companions in the Way, begins to look like common sense. We are units in their mighty procession; and they can teach us how to walk.

*The School of Charity*, pp. 93–4

[ 48 ]

# A Living Organism

When we think of pews and hassocks and the Parish Magazine, we tend to rebel against the yoke of official religion, with its suggestion of formalism and even frowstiness. It seems far too stiff and institutional, too unventilated, to represent the generous and life-giving dealings of the Divine Charity with men and women. The chorus which exclaimed with awe and delight, 'I believe in one God!' thins out a good deal when it comes to saying, 'I believe in one Church!' The first lifted us to heaven; the second brings us down on to the coconut matting with a run. Yet there it is; the Christian sequence is God-Christ-Spirit-Church-Eternal Life. No link in this chain can be knocked out, without breaking the current of love which passes from God through His creatures back again to God. The incarnation of the Holy in this world is social. We are each to contribute our bit to it, and each to depend on the whole. It is not the ardent individual devotee, the supposed recipient of special graces, ruled by special lights and experiences, who is the Bride of Christ. The whole Body is the Bride of Christ: a Body, as St Paul says, having many different members, some of a very odd shape, some of a very lowly kind. And it is in this Body, at once mysterious and homely, that the individual Christian must consent to sink his life, in order that he or she may find true life.

Because of this deep fact of the Living Church, this interconnection of all surrendered spirits, the prayer of one unit can avail for all. We pray as an organism, not as a mere crowd of souls; like grains of rice that happen to be part of the same pudding.

*The School of Charity*, pp. 92–3

# An Essential Service

. . . it is one of the advantages of being a scamp, that one is unable to crystallize into the official shape, and so retains touch with other free lances and realizes how awful the ecclesiastical attitude and atmosphere often makes them feel. As to feeling rather dismayed by the appearance of the Church Visible at the moment – that is inevitable I'm afraid to some extent. But keep your inner eye on the Church Invisible – what the Baron used to call 'the great centralities of religion.' That is what really takes one up into itself 'with angels and arch-angels and all the company of Heaven,' not only the Vicar and the curate and the Mothers' Union Committee. But there is something entrancing, don't you think, in a supernatural society, so wide and generous and really Catholic, that it can mop up all these – even the most depressing – and still remain the Bride of Christ? The Church is an 'essential service' like the Post Office, but there will always be some narrow, irritating and inadequate officials behind the counter and you will always be tempted to exasperation by them.

*To G. F., St Francis, 1932, Letters, pp. 207–8*

# HOMELINESS

'Homeliness' was a term Evelyn Underhill took over from her mentor, Baron von Hügel. It was never meant to be equated exclusively with domesticity and household chores, though the Baron always insisted that home duties should not be neglected in the pursuit of 'holier' diversions, and Evelyn herself made frequent use of analogies from everyday life, particularly 'kitchen' imagery, in her talks and writings. In this she was in good company, for it was the great St Teresa who declared, 'God dwells among the pots and firkins' – which was precisely where the saintly Brother Lawrence spent most of his life.

In the context in which von Hügel, as Evelyn's spiritual director, first introduced the term to her, homeliness was contrasted with – or considered an antidote for – excessive intellectualization. Von Hügel believed that she badly wanted 'de-intellectualizing,' and for this he focussed on two specific areas.

First, the use of her 'spare' time. The Baron was a strong believer in the overall efficacy of 'non-religious' activities: a hobby, an outside interest, or anything contributing to a more leisurely or relaxed change of pace in a too-active life. He suggested to Evelyn that she work amongst the poor in the nearby Kensington slums for two afternoons a week. The contrast with her own sheltered and privileged life stunned her, and later she was to inform the Baron that this had been just what she needed. It had brought her down to earth.

The second area related to her theology, and ultimately to her spirituality. When she went to the Baron for guidance, both her theology and her spirituality were rigidly theocentric. Her concept of God was too dangerously allied with the abstract, remote Neo-Platonist view of deity, and she could not relate to the idea of Christ as God at all. She declared emphatically to von Hügel that she had never prayed to our Lord, and indeed she declared that she never could do so. Von Hügel, one of the leading theologians of the day, perceived that Evelyn was in danger of heresy. Her religious philosophy was not even specifically Christian, although she considered herself to be a Christian. At best, she was a unitarian: one who perceives God as one and rejects the doctrine of the Trinity.

Theological debate was not the appropriate method of effecting a change in her thinking; it would merely have fed her already hyper-intellectual mind and soul. Instead, von Hügel set Evelyn to meditate on Christ in the ordinary activities of his earthly life: first, of course, in his Incarnation, his humble birth. That she was particularly fascinated by the role of the Magi is not at all surprising. They were the intellectuals of their day – but they had much to learn from their contact with the Christ-child. Von Hügel also instructed her to picture Christ's home at Nazareth, his activities on and around the Lake of Galilee, and finally, his death on the Cross, where he showed so much love for all people.

Within a few months, Evelyn knew she was seeing and feeling things in a different light, and that it was the Baron's simple exercise that had effected the change. She wrote: 'Somehow by his prayers he compelled me to experience Christ ... it was like watching the sun rising very slowly. And then suddenly one knew what it was.'[1]

With this change came also a deepened perception and experience of sacramental life, especially the Eucharist. 'I never dreamed it was like this',[2] she told the Baron in awe and gratitude. In an extract in the next section on the Eucharist, Evelyn describes the Eucharist as mixing together, 'the extremes of mystery and homeliness',[3] and provides a most important analogy between ordinary life and sacramental religion; between our relationships with others and 'our secret correspondence with God'.[4] Spiritual selfishness is a bar to genuine communion, both with God and with others.

An incarnational religion, she believed, must be 'drenched in humility'.[5] Directly or indirectly, this lesson is taught in all these extracts. Homeliness is equated with meekness, with becoming as little children, with all the fruits of the Spirit – and with the Cross. Profound truths are conveyed simply – and frequently with a sense of humour! Many of the readings in this book are made more meaningful by Evelyn's tremendous spirit of joy and sense of fun, which is always aligned to common sense and adherence to genuine spiritual priorities.

In 1926, Evelyn wrote to A. B.:

I am sure God has something to teach us in every situation in which we are put, and through every person we meet: and

*once we grasp that, we cease to be restless, and settle down
to learn where we are.*[6]

*These words of advice were reinforced in a later letter to the same
person:*

*Try and see your ordinary daily life as the medium through
which He is teaching your soul, and respond as well as you
can. Then you won't need, in order to receive His lessons, to
go outside your normal experience.*[7]

*The lesson here for all of us is obvious!*

1. Margaret Cropper, *Evelyn Underhill*, p. 83.
2. *ibid.* p. 105.
3. Evelyn Underhill, *Light of Christ*, p. 88.
4. *ibid.* p. 89.
5. Evelyn Underhill, *The Mount of Purification*, p. 26.
6. Charles Williams (ed.), *The Letters of Evelyn Underhill*, p. 173.
7. *ibid.* p. 179.

# Homeliness and Holiness

God in His essential Being is Charity; God so loved that He gave; therefore to dwell in Charity means giving in our turn, a movement of unconditioned generosity which shall be the expression of love. The human soul cuts rather a ridiculous figure, clutching its own bit of luggage, its private treasures, its position, its personality, its rights, over against the holy self-giving of Absolute Love manifest in the flesh. That strange and glimmering Presence, standing on the frontier between the divine and human worlds, attracting and convicting us, asks a total and flexible self-offering as our only possible attitude. 'Christ's human nature,' says the *Theologia Germanica*, 'was so utterly emptied of self and all creatures that it was nothing else but the house, the habitation, the possession of God.' Only thus could the celestial wisdom enter our life.

Why? So that we could know something about Holiness. For no amount of description really tells us anything about Holiness; but an encounter with it shames, amazes, convinces and delights us all at once. 'Thou art the Christ!' says St Peter. 'My Lord and my God!' says St Thomas. They recognize something from beyond the world: One who enters our mixed life in His perfect beauty; and accepts all the normal conditions of an existence which is so much at the mercy of seasons and weather, thirst and hunger, so afflicted by distresses we do not understand, so vexed by devils we cannot cast out and tainted by sins we cannot forget. Through all this that Figure is walking; radiating in and through every situation a selfless charity, an untiring interest and love. The Word has spoken; and spoken in the language of everyday life.

*The School of Charity*, pp. 31–2

# Homeliness and Incarnation

One of the most convicting aspects of Christianity, if we try to see it in terms of our own day, is the contrast between its homely and inconspicuous beginnings and the holy powers it brought into the world. It keeps us in perpetual dread of despising small things, humble people, little groups. The Incarnation means that the Eternal God enters our common human life with all the energy of His creative love, to transform it, to exhibit to us its richness, its unguessed significance; speaking our language, and showing us His secret beauty on our own scale.

Thus the spiritual life does not begin in an arrogant attempt at some peculiar kind of other-worldliness, a rejection of ordinary experience. It begins in the humble recognition that human things can be very holy, full of God; whereas high-minded speculations about His nature need not be holy at all. Since all life is engulfed in Him, He can reach out to us anywhere and at any level. The depth and richness of His Eternal Being are unknown to us. Yet Christianity declares that this unsearchable Life, which is in essence a self-giving Love, and is wholly present wherever it loves, so loved this world as to desire to reveal within it the deepest secret of His thought.

*The School of Charity*, pp. 40–41

[55]

# Homeliness and Self-Abandonment

In the beginning was the Word: and the Word was God, and without Him was not anything made that hath been made: and the Word became flesh and dwelt among us.

That seems immense. A complete philosophy is contained in it. And then we come down to the actual setting of this supreme event, and at once all our notions of the suitable and the significant are set aside; all our pet values reversed. A Baby, just that; and moreover, a Baby born in the most unfortunate circumstances. The extremes of the transcendent and the homely are suddenly brought together in this disconcerting revelation of reality. The hard life of the poor, its ceaseless preoccupation with the lowliest of human needs and duties, and absolute surrender and helplessness, the half-animal status of babyhood; all this is the chosen vehicle for the unmeasured inpouring of the Divine Life and Love. So too the strange simplicity of its beginning both rebukes and reassures us. It is like a quiet voice speaking in our deepest prayer: 'The Lord is with thee' . . . and calling forth the one and only answer, 'Behold the handmaid of the Lord, be it unto me according to thy Word!' Humble self-abandonment is found and declared to be enough to give us God.

*The School of Charity*, pp. 41–2

# Homeliness and the Mystery of Reality

The mystery of Reality enters history very gently by a human channel, and shows the character of Perfect Love within human life; gives us something to hold on to, a Truth which is also a Way and a Life. What we see is not very sensational: but if we look at it steadily, it pierces the heart. First we see a baby, and a long hidden growth; and then the unmeasured outpouring and self spending of an other-worldly love and mercy, teaching, healing, rescuing and transforming, but never trying to get anything for itself. And when we look deeper, we see beyond this a mysterious self-imparting, and a more mysterious anguish and struggle; consummated at last in the most generous and lonely of deaths, issuing in a victory which has given life ever since to all souls. Through this vivid life – what Christ does and how He does it, His prayer, His compassionate healing action, His use of suffering, His communion with God and humankind – the light of Reality floods our twilit inner lives; showing us the human transfigured by the Divine. This is what St Ignatius Loyola intended and desired when he taught his pupils to 'contemplate the Mysteries of the Life of Christ.' Few people do it properly. They are too anxious to get on and be practical: for the lesson of the one thing needful is a lesson which human nature instinctively resists. Yet we shall make our own small work of art all the better if we soak our souls in that beauty first.

*The School of Charity*, pp. 28–9

# Homeliness and Ordinariness

We see the new life growing in secret. Nothing very startling happens. We see the child in the carpenter's workshop. He does not go outside the frame of the homely life in which He appeared. It did quite well for Him, and will do quite well for us; there is no need for peculiar conditions in order to grow in the spiritual life, for the pressure of God's Spirit is present everywhere and at all times. Our environment itself, our home and our job, is the medium through which we experience His moulding action and His besetting love. It is not Christian to try and get out of our frame, or separate our outward life from our life of prayer, since both are the creation of one Charity. The third-rate little town in the hills, with its limited social contacts and monotonous manual work, reproves us when we begin to fuss about our opportunities and our scope. And this quality of quietness, ordinariness, simplicity, with which the saving action of God enters history, endures from the beginning to the end. The child grows like other children, and the lad works like other lads: there is a total abandonment of the individual to the vast Divine purpose, working at its own pace and through ordinary life, and often to us in mysterious ways.

*The School of Charity*, pp. 45–6

# Homeliness and the Humble-Minded

Look at the story of the Magi: those scholars of the ancient world, turning from their abstruse calculations and searching of the heavens because they saw a new star, and driven to seek along fresh paths for a clue to the mystery of life. What they found does not seem at first sight what we should now call 'intellectually satisfying.' It was not a revelation of the Cosmic Mind, but a poor little family party; yet there they were brought to their knees – because, like the truly wise, they were really humble-minded – before a little, living, growing thing. The utmost we can achieve on our own here capitulates before the unspeakable and mysterious simplicity of the method of God; His stooping down to us, His self-disclosure at the very heart of life. After all, the shepherds got there long before the Magi; and even so, the animals were already in position when the shepherds arrived. He comes to His own; the God of our natural life makes of that natural life the very material of His self-revelation. His smile kindles the whole universe; His hallowing touch lies upon all life. The animal world and the natural world have their own rights and their own place within the Thought of God. There never was a religion more deeply in touch with natural things than Christianity, although it is infinite in its scope.

*The School of Charity*, pp. 42–3

# Homeliness and the Christian Mysteries

The essence of the story of the Magi is that it is no use to be too clever about life. Only in so far as we find God in it, do we find any meaning in it. Without Him it is a tissue of fugitive and untrustworthy pleasures, desires, conflicts, frustrations and intolerable pains. Historical Christianity need not involve for us an elaborate philosophy of the Spirit: but it does mean accepting as deeply significant all the great events of the Gospel, because conveying God. And, if we thus recognize the supernatural within these events, some so strange and some so homely; then, we also accept all these incidents as carrying a sacramental reference, conveying something of the over-ruling will and thought of God, and having something in them for each of us. If we are ever to learn all that this record can mean for us, we must never forget that these beyond all other facts of history, are indwelt and moulded by the Divine Charity, are plastic to His creative thought. Everything is there because it conveys spiritual truth in human ways; is a part of all we mean by Incarnation. It all 'speaks to our condition,' as George Fox would say. The Synoptic Gospels may not always have the accuracy of a photograph; but they have a higher realism, because they are charged with God. Like some great work of art, they give us more and more light and food, reveal greater depths of significance, as we grow in that wisdom which is the child of humility and love. That is why meditation on the Christian mysteries, chewing the cud of the Gospels, is so nourishing to the soul, and so inexhaustible as a basis of prayer.

*The School of Charity*, p. 43

# Homeliness and Sturdiness

Our modern religion hardly makes enough of the element [of sturdiness] in the mystery of the Divine revelation; in His pattern declared to humanity, or in the life of prayer. Yet sturdiness, shouldering the burden and accepting the tension inevitable to all great undertakings – getting to grips with the dread problems of life, and the cost of all redemptive action – comes nearer than any fervour to the Mind of Christ, and the demands of Charity. It is comparatively easy for devout minds to feel moved, contrite, exalted, adoring; much more difficult to discount all feelings, and be sturdy about it. Christ was trained in a carpenter's shop; and we persist in preferring a confectioner's shop. But the energy of rescue, the outpouring of sacrificial love, which the supernatural life demands, is not to be got from a diet of devotional meringues and éclairs. The whole life made an oblation from the first – placed on the altar, and lived right through as a reasonable sacrifice from beginning to end – this is the pattern put before us. Only thus can humanity use to the full its strange power of embodying eternal realities; and uniting the extremes of mystery and homeliness.

*The School of Charity*, p. 40

# Homeliness and Hiddenness

We must surely believe that much in Christ's own destiny was deeply mysterious to Him. It seems part of a completed manhood, that He shared our strange human situation, our entire dependence, in this too. The New Testament narrative, with its emphasis on moments when the clouds parted, and He saw His call and what was at work in Him seems to suggest by contrast other, longer stretches; when He looked out from His earthly tabernacle on no clear view, but a path to be trodden in pure abandonment to God. Here again our interior life is conformed to the same pattern. In a general way we must go on steadily, without presuming to demand a clear view. We cannot break the cloud of unknowing in which our lives are folded: like Nicodemus, we must come to Him by night. This should make us realize how deeply hidden, how gradual and unseen by us, the soul's growth in the life of prayer is likely to be. It is like the hidden life at Nazareth. We must be content with the wholesome routine of the nursery, doing ordinary things, learning ordinary lessons and eating ordinary food, if we are to grow truly and organically in wisdom and stature and favour with God and humanity. Growth in God is a far more gradual, less conscious process than we realize at first. We are so raw and superficial in our motions, that we cannot conceive the nature of those tremendous changes by which the child of grace becomes the man or woman of God. We all want to be up and doing long before we are ready to do.

To contemplate the proportions of Christ's life is a terrible rebuke to spiritual impatience and uppish hurry. There we see how slow, according to our time-span, is the maturing of the thought of God. Ephemeral insects become adults in a few minutes, the new-born lamb gets up and starts grazing straight away, but the child depends for months on its mother's love. Sanctity, which is childhood in God, partakes of the long divine duration.

*The School of Charity*, pp. 46–7

# Homeliness is the Fruit of the Spirit

•

Meekness is the grace of the childlike and yet, as a matter of fact, it is the last grace to be added to the mature soul, not the first. We have to become as little children, says Christ. He seems to assume that it will take a lot of doing, and it does. It means measuring our smallness and weakness against the greatness of God, grasping the babyish quality of even our greatest achievements and accepting the situation with delight . . .

Meekness and temperance mean accepting my position, capacities, spiritual *attraits*, as an indication of God's will for me, and not fussing about the things other souls do and feeling despondent because I cannot do them! God hates nothing that He has made. He made it because He liked it. His creation is an act of love. And He has made me perhaps to be a temperate plant and to grow in a temperate climate. So what is required of me is to correspond with that climate and environment and to grow the fruit of His Spirit *here* in the ordinary English garden in which I find myself. No use trying for things which need a tropical climate or a hothouse. We are all rather inclined to be a bit romantic about religion. But God is a realist. He likes home-grown stuff. He asks me for a really good apple, not for a dubious South African peach. So, not lofty thoughts of God, remarkable powers of prayer or displays of devotional fervour or difficult virtues, but gentleness, long-suffering, faithfulness, meekness, a good quality of life, will prove I am growing the right way and producing as well as I can the homely fruit for which He asks.

*The Fruits of the Spirit*, pp. 38, 39

# Homeliness is Creative

You remember when we were children and managed to get into the kitchen, how wonderful it could be with the right kind of cook? A whole world separates the sort who let us watch her make the cake from the sort who let us make a little cake on our own. The intense and solemn interest and joy, the importance of it . . . the whole of our little beings called into action and so satisfied, because we were doing something, making something *real*.

Now in these moments we anticipated the peculiar dignity and privilege of human creatures, those little, half-grown servants of God. We do not merely watch and endure His creative action. We are in our measure allowed to be creative too; we stand by the side of God, making things. How pleased we ought to be, with such a privilege as that. How can we dare to be bored in God's kitchen? Think of this when your part goes a bit slow: when you are set to endless peeling of potatoes or rubbing bread-crumbs through a sieve.

If we are admitted to the privilege of being fellow-workers with God, we must behave accordingly. We must not play with the flour, help ourselves to the sultanas and leave the job half-finished if we get tired. We have got to use the material of life the right way, take it seriously, and do the job as well as we can.

*The Mount of Purification*, p. 79

# Homeliness is Sacramental

The real mark of spiritual triumph – the possession of that more lovely, more abundant life which we discern in moments of deep prayer – is not an abstraction from this world, but a return to it; a willing use of its conditions as material for the expression of love. There is nothing high-minded about Christian holiness. It is most at home in the slum, the street, the hospital ward: and the mysteries through which its gifts are distributed are themselves chosen from amongst the most homely realities of life. A little water, some fragments of bread, and a chalice of wine are enough to close the gap between two worlds; and give soul and senses a trembling contact with the Eternal Charity. By means of these its creatures, that touch still cleanses, and that hand still feels. The serene, unhurried, self-imparting which began before Gethsemane continues still. Either secretly or sacramentally, every Christian is a link in the chain of perpetual penitents and perpetual communicants through which the rescuing Love reaches out to the world. Perhaps there is no more certain mark of a mature spirituality than the way in which those who possess it are able to enter a troubled situation and say, 'Peace,' or turn from the exercise of heroic love to meet the humblest needs of men and women.

*The School of Charity*, p. 67

# Homeliness and Eucharist

The Eucharist is the very heart of Christian worship because it is so rich and far-reaching in its significance; because it eludes thought, eludes emotion, relies on simple contact, humble and childlike receptiveness, sense quenching soul. It mixes together the extremes of mystery and homeliness; takes our common earthly experience of suffering, love, abandonment, death; and makes them inexpressibly holy and fruitful; takes the food of our natural life and transforms that into a channel of Divine Life.

How does our ordinary, homely, everyday life in its spiritual detail harmonize with our Eucharistic practice? Does that consecration lie on the whole of it – family, work, social intercourse, friendship with the poor, intellectual adjustment and public duty, as well as on our secret correspondence with God? Is all that the material of a 'reasonable, holy and living sacrifice'? How do our inward dispositions, our attitude to other people, harmonize with One who comes to us and gives us His very self for love?

The Christian's life is lived in the open, not in a pious cubbyhole. As Christ gives Himself to feed us, so we have to incarnate something of His all-loving, all-sacrificing soul. If we do not, then we have not really received Him. That is the plain truth. It has been said there are many ways and degrees of receiving the Blessed Sacrament. It really depends on how wide we open our hearts. A spiritually selfish communion is not a communion at all. 'Let that mind be in us' which is actually offered to us at the Altar, because it was given to God's purpose on the Cross.

*Light of Christ*, pp. 88–9

# Homeliness and Real Sanctity

It is our own spiritual sloth more than anything else that prevents the whole of our life becoming a sacrament: untidiness that insults the beauty of order; the careless hurry that lets small opportunities of kindness slip; the 'tired feeling' that gradually drops jobs, loses interest in people and causes, when the first excitement dies; the slovenly writing of those letters which are the mysterious link between soul and soul; leaving practical tasks unfinished because we prefer what we call spiritual tasks.

I always have my doubts about the real sanctity of saints who let the pot boil over or forget to sweep the floor. Practical life is for most of us our school of divine service and we are required to bend our whole minds, steadily and quietly, on each thing given us to do. If it is very homely, all the better; *we* are very homely. No one who scamps things will ever find God where He is – in the duties of daily life.

*The Mount of Purification*, pp. 78–9

# TIME GIVEN TO GOD — RETREATS

Evelyn Underhill was tremendously conscious of the tension between work and prayer. On the one hand, she felt the need to unite herself with the redemptive work of Christ which was 'always going on in the world'[1] and which implied direct involvement and intense activity. She demonstrated this through, for example, her work in the slums with the poor. But there was also the other essential side: '. . . one must have the quiet times too, to consolidate that union and stretch out the house of one's soul, and feed on Him.'[2]

For Evelyn, 'the ultimate object of all prayer is greater efficiency for God'.[3] So a time of retreat is not to be equated with sheer self-indulgence and cowardly escapism, but must be regarded as a practical and spiritual necessity.

Evelyn attended her first conducted retreat at Pleshey Retreat House in March 1922, and it profoundly influenced her spiritual life, her view of institutional religion, and her relationships with her fellow Christians. She wrote to her spiritual director, Baron von Hügel:

> The intense silence seemed to slow down one's far too quick mental time and give one's soul a chance. To my surprise a regime of daily Communion and four services a day with silence between was the most easy unrestrained and natural life I had ever lived. One sank down into it, and doing it always with the same people, all meaning it intensely, and the general attitude of deep devotion – for the whole house seemed soaked in love and prayer – cured solitude and gave me at last the feeling of belonging to the Christian family and not counting except as that. I . . . gained a wholly new sense of the realness and almost unbearable beauty of the Christian life.[4]

Exactly two years later, she conducted her first retreat – also at Pleshey. It was a bold and innovative move – to our knowledge, no laywoman had ever before conducted a retreat in the Anglican Church. It is all the more significant that she was asked to do it – she did not seek it out; and such was her success that thereafter *she remained in demand, taking seven or eight retreats a year until poor health forced the reduction, and finally the cessation, of this work. Many of her works published from 1924 onwards (including some posthumous works) are actually compilations of these retreats, exactly as she had given them:* Concerning the Inner Life *(1926);* The House of the Soul *(1929);* The School of Charity *(1934);* The Mystery of Sacrifice *(1938);* Abba *(1940);* The Fruits of the Spirit *(1942);* Light of Christ *(1944). More recently, Grace Brame has unearthed a series of previously unpublished early retreats which she has published under the title,* The Ways of the Spirit *(1990).*

*Evelyn regarded the revival of the retreat as one of the most important results of the Oxford Movement; but in fact she herself probably played an even more significant part in the extension of this work. In 1913 there was only one retreat house servicing the entire Anglican Church. By 1932 there were 22 Diocesan Houses (of which Pleshey was one), and over 30 belonging to religious communities. Some of these accommodated over a thousand retreatants a year. During the Second World War many of them, for obvious practical reasons, closed down; but it was a great source of comfort to Evelyn that Pleshey survived and continued to flourish – as indeed it still does today.*

*Evelyn always stressed to her retreatants the importance of silence and what a retreat really meant; some of the following extracts are taken from those retreats. They witness to her own priorities: in retreat, we come to be with God, God first and God alone.*

1. Christopher Armstrong, *Evelyn Underhill*, p. 222.
2. *ibid.* p. 223.
3. Evelyn Underhill, *Collected Papers*, p. 46.
4. Margaret Cropper, *Evelyn Underhill*, p. 87.

# Making a True Retreat

We all know pretty well why we come into Retreat: we come to seek the opportunity of being alone with God and attending to God, in order that we may do His will better in our everyday lives. We have come to live for a few days in the life of prayer and deepen our contact with the spiritual realities on which our lives depend – to recover if we can our spiritual poise. We do not come for spiritual information, but for spiritual food and air – to wait on the Lord and renew our strength – not for our own sakes but for the sake of the world.

'Thou when thou prayest, enter into thy closet – and *shut the door.*' I think we can almost see the smile with which Christ said those three words: and those three words can define what we have to try to do. Anyone can retire into a quiet place and have a thoroughly unquiet time in it – but that is not making a Retreat! It is the shutting of the door which makes the whole difference between a true Retreat and a worried religious weekend.

Christ said Shut, and He meant Shut. A complete barrier deliberately set up, with you on one side along with God and everything else without exception on the other side. The voice of God is very gentle; we cannot hear it if we let other voices compete. Our ordinary life, of course, is not lived like that and should not be; but this bit of life is to be lived like that. It is no use at all to enter that closet, that inner sanctuary, clutching the daily paper, the reports of all the societies you support, your engagement book and a large bundle of personal correspondence. All these must be left outside. The motto for your Retreat is *God only*, God in Himself, sought for Himself alone.

*The Fruits of the Spirit*, pp. 1–2

# Centring Down

The object of Retreat is not Intercession or self-exploration, but such communion with Him as shall afterwards make you more powerful in intercession; and such self-loss in Him as shall heal your wounds by new contact with His life and love.

You would hardly enter the presence of the human being you most deeply respected and loved in the state of fuss and preoccupation and distraction in which we too often approach God. You are to 'centre down' as the Quakers say, into that deep stillness which is the proper atmosphere of your soul. Remain with God. Wait upon the Light . . . Speak to your Heavenly Father who is in secret. These are the words that describe the attitude of the soul really in Retreat. Do not think now of the world's state and needs and sufferings or of your problems and responsibilities; this is not the time for that. Do not think too much about your own sins. A general, humble, but very tranquil act of penitence and acknowledgement of your faultiness is best. 'Commune with your Father which is in secret.' There is always something dark, hidden, secret, about our real intercourse with God. In religion we should always distrust the obvious and the clear. The closet where we speak to Him is not very well lit – but the light that filters into it has a quality of its own; it is a ray of the Eternal Light on which we cannot easily look: but as we get used to it, sun ourselves in its glow, we learn, as we can bear it, to see more and more. Therefore we must be content to dwell with God in that dim silence. Gaze at Him *darkly*, as the mystics say, offer yourselves again and again to Him. 'All Friends everywhere,' said Fox, 'keep all your meetings, *waiting* on the Light' – a perfect prescription for a good Retreat.

*The Fruits of the Spirit*, pp. 2–3

# Our Need of Retreat

A first retreatant lately told me that when she confessed to her husband what she intended to do, he took his pipe from his mouth and said earnestly: 'Go, my dear. Go by all means! You're just about due for a spot of re-birth.' That man, it seems to me, had a very clear idea of one function of a retreat: its power of causing the re-birth of our spiritual sense, quickening that which has grown dull and dead in us, calling it out into light and air, giving it another chance.

Most of us are bitterly conscious of the extent in which we are at the mercy of our surroundings: which grow ever more and more insistent in their pressure, their demands on our attention and time; less and less suggestive of reality, of God. They call out and keep out the least spiritual side of our nature: and almost insensibly, often with the very best intentions, and under plea of good works, family duties, social obligations, we capitulate to the surface activities of existence, the ceaseless chain of passing events. We forget that awestruck upward glance which is the mark of the spiritual person. Then we lose all sense of proportion; become fussy, restless, full of things that simply must be done, quite oblivious of the only reason why anything should be done. Our prayers become more and more like supernatural shopping lists, less and less like that conversation between one friend and another which is the ideal of Thomas à Kempis. We can't rest in the Lord; there really isn't time for that. Besides, there's the telephone, which may be trusted to ring at the most shattering moment. So we gradually forget what interior silence is like, and seldom enter the interior world: and the result of this is appreciated only too well by all those with whom we have to deal. When we have reached this stage, nothing is going to save us but that Spot of Re-birth. We need a re-quickening of the spark of the soul; a re-emergence of the 'fine point of the spirit' – that most sacred and least considered element of human personality, so easily shoved down into the cellar, smothered and forgotten in the pressure of practical everyday life.

'The Need of Retreat', from *The Vision*, January 1932, pp. 3–4

# To Let the Soul Speak

Our so-called civilization gets more and more complicated, more and more noisy. It is like one of those mills where the noise of the looms makes it impossible for the workers to hear each other speak. And if we go on at it long enough without a break we begin to think the looms are all that matter, and we are merely there to keep them going and must not bother about anything else. In other words, I am sure there is a real danger that Christian spirituality in its deepest and loveliest reaches will be killed out by the pressure and demands of the social machine, and even of the ecclesiastical machine. We will get ever more utilitarian and this-world, and will wholly forget our true relation to God. I am sure you remember the beautiful letter of Baron von Hügel, in which he tells his pupil how all that we do has a double relatedness. It is part of the chain of cause and effect which makes up human life; and also it is, or can be, joined directly to God, the Changeless Reality who gives meaning to that life. To realize, make, keep up that double connection – this is to be fully human, fully alive; and how are we to teach and establish that in the scutter of the modern world? Even religion tends to become more and more pragmatic, utilitarian; more and more active, and less and less inward; more and more of a chain of doings, less and less of an attachment, a being. And so by a curious paradox, as our physical universe gets larger, our true horizon shrinks. We have become the slave of the clattering loom. We can't hear our own souls speak.

Now those who control the modern factory – wiser in their generation than the children of light – know what all this means in the exhausting and impoverishing of human material in nervous tension, apathy, unrest. So there is no good factory without its welfare department, its rest room, its opportunity for quiet. To withdraw the worker at times from the clatter and pressure is to increase the quantity and quality of the work. So I sometimes think retreats should be regarded as a bit of spiritual welfare work; quite essential to the organization of the Church.

'The Need of Retreat', from *The Vision*, January 1932, pp. 4–5

# A Rest Most Busy

I don't mean to recommend the retreat for merely practical reasons – because it makes the effective active Christian even more active and effective than before. I would rather recommend it because it puts in the foreground and keeps in the foreground that which is, after all, the first interest of religion – so easily lost sight of – the one thing needful – the soul's relation to God. That relation is so subtle, so invisible, so deeply personal, and yet so powerful – how is its delicate beauty to be savoured, and its humbling influence felt, while Martha runs from the gas-stove to the scullery, listening with one ear to the loud-speaker declaiming morning prayers? We need for that such a silence and leisure as we get in a good retreat; what one of the mystics called a 'rest most busy.' Then the repressed elements of our truest being can emerge and get light and air; and perhaps such a renewal of faith, hope and charity – those three virtues that are trained wholly towards God – that they may keep their heads above water when re-immersed in the torrent of the world.

I believe the retreat as a part of our normal spiritual routine will yield on the whole its fullest results when we regard it more often and more generally, in Abbot Delatte's beautiful phrase, as an opportunity of 'steeping our souls in the beauty of the mysterious.' To dwell quietly and without self-occupation in the atmosphere of God is surely the best of all ways of redressing the balance between the temporal and eternal sides of our life. It is this aspect of the retreat experience which seems to me to deepen, steady and enrich personality; it is this which produces the 'Spot of Re-birth,' and sends the retreatant back to the world more able to find the inward in the outward than before. In relation to this aspect, and the production of this atmosphere, the conductor has a special responsibility; for nothing that he does here will be of the slightest use to his retreatants, unless it proceeds from his or her own interior life with God.

'The Need of Retreat', from *The Vision*, January 1932, pp. 5–6

# Contemplation of Christ

We have added something else to the object of our Retreat: it is a time when we can listen to the secret whisper of the Spirit and look at Christ again, for the contemplation of Christ is the first part of Christianity. One will help the other, enrich the other. The doctrine of the Trinity means that many-sided revelation of God and expression of God.

A time like this can be such a rich experience if we take it the right way – open up our souls, open our spiritual ears and eyes to the 'beauty of the Mystery.' Don't let us waste all the time merely examining our own state! If we look steadily and humbly at Christ's life and see in it the truth about human life and especially our own lives as His servants and fellow-workers, each time we look we shall find ourselves shrinking by contrast and at last we shall be so small we shall become as little children. Nothing could be better than that!

Contemplation of Christ does not mean an emotional sort of pious day-dream; it means entering by a deliberate, self-oblivious and humble attention into the tremendous mysteries of His Life – mysteries which each give us some deep truth about the Life and Will of God and the power and vocation of a soul that is given to God – mysteries which each one of us in particular is called to make part of our very lives. They will break up, into colours we can deal with, that white light of God's Holiness at which we cannot look.

*Light of Christ*, pp. 2–7

# The Windows of Holiness

You know how Plato spoke of this life as a cave in which men were imprisoned and could only judge reality by seeing the shadow cast by light outside. But for Christians the cave has become a great shrine in which we are taught and moulded for the purpose of our creation – a sacrificial life in union with God. We come here to recapture that vision; to open up our unsatisfactory little souls to the light that pours in through the windows of His holiness. One glance round this evening is quite enough to fill us with that loving penitence for the past and that generous courage for the future which are the best of all dispositions for entering a Retreat.

We will take it all very quietly and humbly, try to leave our arguing, critical selves behind. Christianity is not an argument and Christianity is not given us in the form of logic but in the form of beauty and love. We must be receptive, humble and quiet.

Perhaps we shall see a beauty we have not yet seen or guessed before. The treasure hidden in the field was a great treasure; there is something there for everyone. Don't let us spoil our piece by trying to change it into ordinary currency and then grousing about the exchange.

*Light of Christ*, pp. 30–1

# The Open Door

It sometimes happens that one goes to see a cathedral which is famous for the splendour of its glass; only to discover that, seen from outside, the windows give us no hint whatever of that which awaits us within. They all look alike; dull, thick, and grubby. From this point of view we already realize that they are ancient, important, the proper objects of reverence and study. But we cannot conceive that solemn coloured mystery, that richness of beauty, and meaning which is poured through them upon those who are inside the shrine. Then we open the door, and go inside. We leave the outer world and enter the inner world; and at once we are surrounded by a radiance, a beauty, that lie beyond the fringe of speech. The universal Light of God in which we live and move, and yet which in its reality always escapes us, pours through those windows; bathes us in an inconceivable colour and splendour, and shows us things of which we never dreamed before.

In the same way, the deep mysteries of the Being of God and the call of the soul cannot be seen by us, until they have passed through a human medium, a human life. Nor can that life, and all that it means as a revelation of God, His eternal truth and beauty, be realized by us from the outside. One constantly hears people commenting on Christianity, passing judgment on Christianity; and missing the point every time, because they are on the wrong side of the wall. It is only within the place of prayer, recollection, worship and love, the place where the altar is and where sacrifice is made, that we can cleanse our vision, overcome our self-interested bias, and fully and truly receive the revelation of Reality which is made to us in Christ.

*The School of Charity*, p.27

# Transmitters of Power

So here we stand at the end of our Retreat and ask, 'How, so far, has my heart, soul, mind, strength, my secret prayer and outer service played its part as a unit of the Body of Christ? What has it done to further His teaching, healing, rescuing, sacrificial work? How have my God-given energies contributed to the purposes of God?'

None of us can hope to do much in *all* these departments; some are called to one, some to another. Not all are teachers, not all can pour out that living and beautiful compassion which heals the wounds of life; not all are allowed to be with Christ on the Cross. But we each have our place and job in His economy; it is a triumph of balanced energy and deep peace.

Does the light of the window illuminate my special powers and opportunities? Perhaps they may lie specially in one of these departments, or perhaps in a humble, supple, self-giving life which keeps open in prayer the channel of love and finds place for something of each. Christ's Spirit, if I let it, can act through mine – praying in me and above me as St Patrick said – and I was given to Him in baptism and gave myself to Him again of my own free will *for* this purpose, to be one more transmitter of God's power and love.

*Light of Christ*, p. 95

# Towards Sanctification

And finally, what is to be the real objective – the aim – which we who believe in the retreat movement set before ourselves?

The object is the same as the object of the Christian life – sanctity – the production, fostering and maintenance of holiness. To sanctify, as von Hügel was fond of saying, is the biggest thing out. Now souls are sanctified by the pressure and cleansing action of the Spirit, acting through and in the events of everyday life. But in order that the action of the Spirit may produce this effect, we know that a particular disposition, outlook, temper, is also required in the soul. And how is that to be produced? Perhaps most easily and directly by taking the soul from its normal preoccupations and placing it in an atmosphere and condition in which, with the minimum of distraction, it can attend to and realize God. And this in essence is a retreat.

Isn't it worth while to make some effort to create and keep going houses in which so great a thing can be done? Our increased capitulation to pace and noise makes it more and more necessary to provide such opportunities for realizing our spiritual status, and learning the width of the chasm which separates deep from distracted prayer. It is not easy under everyday conditions to learn and maintain the art of steadfast attention to God; yet no art could more certainly serve His purposes than this. 'One loving spirit sets another on fire.' The Church will win the world for Christ when – and when only – she works through living spirits steeped in prayer.

'The Need of Retreat', from *The Vision*, January 1932, pp. 6–7

# THE EUCHARIST

The Vatican Documents describe the Eucharist as the 'summit and source' of worship, and to this principle, thirty years earlier, Evelyn Underhill had soundly ascribed. Her book, Worship, published in 1936, was one of the most important products of a period in which many of the major Churches were establishing a basis for liturgical reform, and for ecumenical dialogue as a consequence of this, within their own ranks.

However, we know from the previous chapter on homeliness that Evelyn had encountered great personal difficulties in reaching an adequate understanding and, more importantly, a deep experience of the Eucharist. When she finally did, it was so awesome, so beautiful, and so intensely personal that it was 'quite undiscussible'[1] – even with the Baron.

This 'purely spiritual' aspect must never be lost or submerged in theological debate. When that happens, the Eucharist becomes a source of division, not unity. Evelyn saw the Eucharist as the paradigm of all Christian worship, and the five principles she lists are deprived of their full meaning if they are ever detached from our understanding of our relationship with God or our relationship with others.

Evelyn's guidelines for the Eucharist – and all worship – are laid down in Worship, pp. 246–50. It should be:

1 THEOCENTRIC: 'hallowed and penetrated by a sense of the Transcendence of God'.

2 INCARNATIONAL: 'accepting and consecrating to its purposes both worlds, of sense and spirit'.

3 Essentially CHRISTOCENTRIC: 'the realistic continuance in liturgical form of the primitive Christian mystery of communion with the risen Christ'.

4 Fundamentally, though not exclusively, SACRIFICIAL: 'In it, the Church, the Body of Christ, accepts her vocation . . . [and] is consecrated to His redeeming purposes . . .'

5 Thoroughly SOCIAL and ORGANIC: intensely corporate ('The

*Catholic Christian does not or should not go to the Eucharist
on an individual errand, even of the most spiritual kind'); its
outward rites and symbols declaring 'a hidden supernatural
order, where all things are united in God'.*

In her own time, Evelyn saw the Eucharist being restored to a
more central position in the worship of many of the Protestant
denominations – especially in the Anglican Church. She witnessed
the Roman Catholic Church endeavouring to restore the primitive
balance and integrity of the Mass as a truly corporate act of
worship with greater congregational participation, audibly recited
prayers, the Gospel in the vernacular, and the restoration of the
Offertory procession. More frequent reception of Holy Communion was an acknowledgement of the interdependence between
God and His people, and essentially part of the rhythm of the
spiritual life, which Evelyn viewed as Eucharistic and thus sacrificial. Like Augustine and some of the early Church Fathers, she
identified all life with the Eucharist: 'The whole of life is to be
eucharisticized . . . It is to be offered, blessed, and made the vehicle
of that infinite self-giving.'[2] This, inevitably, means suffering and
the Cross – or at least the willingness to accept them, if they are
the 'chalice of Christ' which is designated for us.

The selections on the Eucharist which follow are not chosen on
the grounds of theological profundity – though they are indisput-
ably sound doctrine – but for their ability to convey the awesome
and the ordinary; the transcendent and the homely; the profound
and the humble; the generosity of God, and the joyful anticipation
of the 'free heart' awaiting 'the invasion of Love'.

The process is ongoing. Evelyn reminds us that we are 'perpetual
communicants' – 'there is no other way of carrying on' other than
in Christ's presence, where there is 'fullness of joy'.[3] That joy and
gratitude should overwhelm us: that is true Eucharist!

1. Margaret Cropper, *Evelyn Underhill*, p. 92.
2. Evelyn Underhill, *The Mystery of Sacrifice*, pp. 65–6.
3. Evelyn Underhill, *Light of Christ*, pp. 87–8.

# What is the Eucharist?

The Eucharist is the characteristic act towards God and towards the whole Church: a great movement of adoring gratitude, an offering to Him of natural and to them of supernatural gifts, a deep participation in the self-given life of the Divine Charity. And in the Eucharist the principal and invisible actor, 'Priest and Victim' in the ancient language of the Liturgy, is Christ, whose members we are. Thus in the Prayer of Humble Access we are really asking for full participation in the life of the Church, with all the mysterious privileges and the solemn obligations of those who are, as St Ambrose says, 'made partakers of the Supreme Divinity'.

It is true that such a vocation in its wholeness is far too much for most of us. It can only be a corporate undertaking. Not all can contemplate the Eternal Realities, or enter into the awful mystery of the Cross. But all – including the large and endearing class of spiritual tweenies, ever ready to help with any job – have some place and task within that economy; the triumph of balanced energy and eternal peace. We must be ready for whatever bit falls to our own share – probably not the bit that we expected or desired – and in our secret life towards God, must be so humble, supple, and self-giving, so austere in our demands, that we are kept in training for the test, and wide open to that Spirit who is both the transformer and the ruler of those to whom He comes in power. This lays a great responsibility on every Christian; for it means that our self-discipline, our prayer, our renunciations, our struggles, are not undertaken merely for our own sakes. They are required of us, in order that we may be made more fit for this great vocation, and so increase the energy of the Church. The shallow notion of the life of prayer as a form of spiritual selfishness wilts before this vision of the destiny of the awakened soul.

*The School of Charity*, pp. 98–9

# Free and Unconditional Self-Offering

As He drew near to the crisis of the Passion, Jesus said to His disciples, 'I have a baptism to be baptized with; and how am I straitened till it be accomplished!' Limited, held in, narrowed in action and in power. The baptism to which He looked for liberation was the death, the entire self-giving of the Cross; after it was accomplished He was no longer straitened but free, transformed. Thus the sacrifice completed upon Calvary was not a tragedy, but a release: the gate of entrance to a wide-spreading life and unlimited redeeming power. So too, in its own measure, and according to the courage and completeness of its self-oblation, the soul can enter the sacrificial order, can cease to be straitened, accept in its fullness and cost the true vocation of humanity, and be consecrated to the redeeming and creative purposes of God.

The beginning of that Eucharistic life which is the true life of the Church and each of her members, is such a free and unconditional self-offering of the created life to that transforming energy which is even now at work on us. We are to offer in simplicity what we are and what we have to the eternal purposes of God; without any self-occupied attempt to determine its precise quality and value. The soul, says St John of the Cross, is like an unopened parcel. Only God knows what He has put in it, and wherein its ordained perfection consists: self-scrutiny at its best hardly gets beyond the paper and the string. The meek adoring self-oblivious attitude, the generous gesture, the cost, are the things that matter; not the particular form or apparent value of the gift. The oblation may seem small and homely; may bear none of the outward marks of religion. It is none the less an earnest of love, and so a part of the raw material of the eternal Eucharist.

*The Mystery of Sacrifice*, pp. 20–1

# Transforming Charity

The Church offers herself for all in a great movement of cherishing love; brings them and their needs with her to the altar. 'To *all* thy people give thy heavenly grace!' No class, no type is excluded. The dower of the supernatural is asked for all. The desire for God, which is the essential disposition of the awakened heart, is here completed by the Christian, all-loving, desire for souls. At the Church's altar, Eros and Agape meet. For the action of the Liturgy has a universal quality. In it we seek to bring all creation within the radius of transforming Charity. Almost in one breath, as it were, we offer all and we ask all; confiding the total interests of all men and women to the creative love which is so deeply interested in them, and bringing all life with us in our humble movement towards heavenly places that it may be eucharisticized, made more susceptible to God, more amenable to the secret pressures of His Will.

*The Mystery of Sacrifice*, p. 30

# A Generous Oblation

Now we are to go up to heavenly places, to the altar of sacrifice, bearing our humble gifts. As in the primitive Church the worshippers carried up to the altar their homely oblations of bread and wine for the Mysteries, so the soul's movement towards God must begin with an act which opposes its ingrained possessiveness, and of which it bears the cost. Something which we feel to be our own – though indeed we have nothing – must be given at our own expense and of our own free will. Like children in the nursery, we are taught generosity by the making of little gifts; and so prepared for that total and mutual gift in which alone our lives are made complete.

The offering is made ungrudgingly and with gladness. It does not represent an impoverishment, but a fulfilment of life. 'The people rejoiced for that they offered willingly to the Lord,' says the Chronicler, as he narrates the bringing in of the materials which were to build on Mount Zion a Temple for the habitation of God. Here the created is lifted up, that it may become the dwelling-place of the Uncreated and so achieve the purpose for which it was made. For the spirit of oblation is the direct enemy of the spirit of self-love, and its practice is the most perfect mortification of self-love. The Church and the soul do not go to the altar preoccupied with their own needs and desires, but with the pure Glory of God. Their offering, even though it shall minister to them the Food of Eternity, is primarily a gift made to God; and joy, the temper of Reality, rewards this small gesture of love.

Thus oblation is the very stuff of prayer.

*The Mystery of Sacrifice*, pp. 16, 17

# The Most Costly Sacrifice

The history of the soul is marred throughout its course by cheap and unworthy oblations, which look impressive, but have not cost enough; by efforts to elude the price of holiness, the totality of its obligation to God. The real gift may not look its value; but it is bought, like the Pearl and the Field, with all that we have.

Thus the theme of sacrifice will receive in each soul a separate and distinct interpretation; conditioned by its possessions, its vision, its temper, courage and limitations. It is within the circumstances of our life that we shall find the stuff of our oblation. 'We are His sacrifice, and the offering is only the symbol of what we really are', says St Augustine again. Character in all its manifestations; our habitual thoughts and actions, our interests and our work, our aims and our relationships, our everyday routine, are here to be unselfed and orientated towards eternity; made part of the eternal sacrifice which the created order offers in Christ to God, and thus given a new worth and a new significance. The tension and conflicts which exhaust the soul arise from its implicit resistance to this, its real destiny: the pull of personal desire, the pressure of self-will, the taint of possessiveness, the arrogant reluctance to accept the homely and commonplace as the appointed material of its spiritual offering. And with this, the refusal to undertake those delicate and difficult adjustments which shall place the focus of its being where alone stability is to be found, and bring it into the deep and active peace of the unified and surrendered will.

Perhaps the most costly sacrifice the self is here required to make, is its own cherished idea of the creature that it wished to be and to offer ... Sooner or later that attractive picture of our spiritual situation goes to the altar. Then the soul, stripped of all the garments and disguises which ministered to its secret self-love, sees itself in its shabbiness and emptiness, its mere human second-ratedness. Clad only in that self-knowledge it stands alone before the Holy, to offer the one thing that matters; the oblation of a free heart, cleansed of delusions, images and attachments, truly poor, truly chaste, truly obedient, and therefore ready for the invasion of love.

*The Mystery of Sacrifice*, pp. 23–4

# The Flame of Living Charity

The Liturgy declares again and again that once we have entered the supernatural region it is God alone who is the mover, the doer of all that is done. He alone uplifts, renews, transforms, converts, consecrates by the independent action of His grace; and this His consecrating action is mostly unperceived by us. His invisible rays beat upon, penetrate, and transform the soul. Sometimes their action quietens and steadies us; sometimes it burns and convicts us, and produces profound religious discomfort which we do not understand. But the full power of those transforming rays could not be endured by us at all, if it rose to the level of consciousness and was felt by sensitive nature. The saints have sometimes spoken of it; of the awful burning of the Fire of Love, the flame of living charity that burns to heal, or the agony of the heat that purifies our desire, cleanses the thoughts of the heart, scorches and kills self-esteem. This is the real fire that burns on the altar, and into which the living sacrifice must be plunged.

*The Mystery of Sacrifice*, pp. 44–5

# The Joy of Welcoming Love

How completely the liturgic pattern rebukes those who come to religion for the sake of their own souls; and, valuing its sacraments as means to the satisfaction of their own spiritual needs, ignore both their corporate responsibility in respect of the whole Eucharistic action, and the place of that whole action in the vast economy of God. For here the small self-offering of men and women in their wholeness is met by the Divine generosity; and transformed to His supernatural purpose; and the separate experiences of individual devotion are to be esteemed only as fragments of this one sublime experience of the Bride of Christ. Thus it is only when costly and humble adoration, lost in the tide of worship and bowed down before that which it can never understand, has reached its height, that the soul can draw near to receive the food of Eternal Life. Then, the joy of giving is met and completed by the joy of welcoming love. By a series of profound contemplations, expressed in dramatic action and disclosing each aspect of her relation to God, the Church has moved towards communion with Him. So too, in so far as the individual life is concerned, it is only those who have accepted the long, exacting discipline of preparation, who have offered themselves in oblation, given themselves to intercession and finally surrendered all to the triune consecrating Power, who can enter into the depth and fullness of that mysterious communion in which they feed upon the self-given Divine life.

*The Mystery of Sacrifice*, pp. 59–60

# The Christian Communicant

There is a type of ancient picture which shows all the Sacraments centred in and dependent from the Cross: the love self-given there giving itself for ever to all, the undying source of grace and purification and truth. It is a wonderful image of what the Christian Church and Christian life really are, a continuation of the Incarnation. It reminds us that the Spirit of Christ is now living and truly present with and in His Church, His Family, His Mystic Body, and, because of His one eternal sacrifice ever giving us His life, and that we are utterly and entirely dependent on that life as branches on the Vine, His touch still cleansing us, His hand still feeding us. Either secretly or sacramentally all living Christians are perpetual penitents and perpetual communicants, there is no other way of carrying on. The Eucharist represents a perpetual pouring out of His very life to feed and enhance our small and feeble lives. Think only of that as we kneel before the window of His Passion and a wonderful joy and gratitude tempers our shame.

Now turn and look at ourselves, our own lives, in the light of this revelation of the Charity of God. What courage, what humility, what absolute self-giving it requires of us if we are to be the channels through which that mysterious life is to be poured out on others, and that is what it means to be Members of Christ. In Holy Communion we pledge ourselves to that – 'the fellowship of His sufferings' . . . 'In Thy presence is fullness of joy.' Consider how drastically our idea of joy must be purified, how saturated with sacrificial love, before we can drink of the chalice of Christ.

*Light of Christ*, pp. 87–8

# PRAYER

For Evelyn, prayer is adoration; and because the object of prayer is union with God, the nature and purpose of our relationship with him are clearly defined. Everything we do is placed in this perspective: of God and the priority of God, and of our littleness and great need of him. We come to his outstretched hand and we take what he gives us. Prayer is our acknowledgement of our entire dependence on God; complete surrender is essential, for those who pray become 'the self-emptied channels of the only Wonderful – the Mighty God, the Everlasting Father.'[1]

It follows that any prayer which focuses on oneself and encourages one to revel in 'mere devotionalism', or produces emotional strain or spiritual inertia, is not genuine prayer. Our prayer time is not a cosy time for daydreaming about ourselves, but the opportunity for contemplating the life of Christ, and offering ourselves to be used in whatever way he pleases.

The realization of God's presence may or may not be a side-effect of prayer: but a more essential part is being prepared to plod on, even in the dark. 'Your chief prayer', Evelyn told one of her directees, 'must not be to "see Him first and always", but to be useful to Him first and always!'[2] Thus prayer expands one 'from a narrow individuality' to 'a personality capable of being fully used on supernatural levels for supernatural work.'[3]

Indeed, prayer has power: 'one human spirit can, by its prayer and love, touch and change another human spirit.'[4] But Evelyn reminds us firmly that the power is God's, not ours, and God's power can transform the most ordinary and homely into the supernatural.

This, for those who surrender themselves to co-operate with God, is 'the state of holiness'.[5]

1. Evelyn Underhill, *Light of Christ*, p. 75.
2. Charles Williams (ed.), *The Letters of Evelyn Underhill*, p. 188.
3. Evelyn Underhill, *Man and the Supernatural*, p. 203.
4. Evelyn Underhill, *Collected Papers*, p. 83.
5. Evelyn Underhill, *Man and the Supernatural*, p. 203.

# What is Prayer (1)

What, after all, is prayer? It is a mutual act, a communion of the created spirit with Uncreated Spirit: of the human self, immersed in contingency and succession, with the all-penetrating God who yet transcends contingency and succession – in whom, as St Augustine said, 'are all moments of time.' It is therefore the religious act *par excellence;* and rightly understood, should give us a clue to all that religion means in life. 'We know in general,' says Grou, 'that prayer is a religious act; but when it comes to praying, we easily lose sight of the fact that it is a supernatural act, which is consequently beyond our power, and which we cannot properly perform without the inspiration and help of grace.' The initiative then, in all genuine prayer, is not human but Divine. And next, I think, we must add that this communion of spirit with Spirit to which we are mysteriously urged, and which more and more dominates those lives that are becoming sensitive to God, is purposive. It always looks beyond itself to some further creative goal – great or small, general or particular, remote or immediate – to be achieved by this collaboration of Divine and human will and desire. If we give a sufficiently wide and deep content to our terms, this will be found on analysis to be true even of the most apparently passive and formless prayer of contemplation, which seems to the praying soul to be no more than the expression of its own thirst for surrender, and merely to place it at the disposal of God. For since the ultimate goal of the immanent Divine Will must be the supernaturalization of all life, and prayer is a sovereign means through which the Divine Immanence works, we cannot deny the purposive nature of such passive and generalized prayer.

Its creative goal, however, may be concerned with almost any level or aspect of physical or spiritual life; for the prayer of a wide-open and surrendered human spirit appears to be a major channel for the free action of that Spirit of God with whom this soul is 'united in her ground.'

'Thoughts on Prayer and the Divine Immanance', from
*The Expository Times,* June 1931, p. 405

# What is Prayer (2)

Prayer is, if not the guarantee, at least a mighty witness to the reality of the spiritual life. If we were merely clever animals, had no kinship with God, we could not pray: no communion between Him and us would be possible. Prayer in its three great forms of Worship, Communion and Intercession, is after all, a purely spiritual activity; an acknowledgement of the supreme reality and power of the spiritual life. As St Thomas says, it is a 'marvellous intercourse between Infinite and finite, God and the soul'.

If the first term of the spiritual life is recognition in some way or other of the splendour and reality of God, the first mood of prayer – the ground from which all the rest must grow – is certainly worship, awe, adoration; delight in that holy reality for its own sake. This truth has lately returned to the foreground of religious thought; and there is little need to insist on it afresh. Religion, as von Hügel loved to say, *is* adoration; our humble acknowledgement of the Transcendent, the Fact of God – the awestruck realism of the seraphs in Isaiah's vision – the meek and loving sense of mystery which enlarges the soul's horizon and puts us in our own place! Prayer, which is so much more a state and condition of soul than a distinct act, begins there; in the lifting of the eyes of the little creature to the Living God, or perhaps to the symbol through which the Living God reveals Himself to the soul.

*Mixed Pasture*, pp. 53–4

# The Meaning of Prayer

Prayer means turning to Reality, taking our part, however humble, tentative and half-understood, in the continual conversation, the communion, of our spirits with the Eternal Spirit; the acknowledgement of our entire dependence, which is yet the partly free dependence of the child. For Prayer is really our whole life toward God: our longing for Him, our 'incurable God-sickness,' as Barth calls it, our whole drive towards Him. It is the humble correspondence of the human spirit with the Sum of all Perfection, the Fountain of Life. No narrower definition than this is truly satisfactory, or covers all the ground. Here we are, small half-real creatures of sense and spirit, haunted by the sense of a Perfection ever calling to us, and yet ourselves so fundamentally imperfect, so hopelessly involved in an imperfect world; with a passionate desire for beauty, and more mysteriously still, a knowledge of beauty, and yet unable here to realize perfect beauty; with a craving for truth and a deep reverence for truth, but only able to receive flashes of truth. Yet we know that perfect goodness, perfect beauty, and perfect truth exist within the Life of God; and that our hearts will never rest in less than these. This longing, this need of God, however dimly and vaguely we feel it, is the seed from which grows the strong, beautiful and fruitful plant of prayer. It is the first response of our deepest selves to the attraction of the Perfect; the recognition that he has made us for Himself, that we depend on Him and are meant to depend on Him, and that we shall not know the meaning of peace until our communion with Him is at the centre of our lives.

*The Spiritual Life*, pp. 56–7

# Union With God

The life of the spirit is an organic process, a continuous Divine action; not a sudden miracle or a series of jerks. Therefore there should be no struggle, impatience, self-willed effort in our prayer and self-discipline; but rather a great flexibility, a homely ordered life, a gentle acceptance of what comes to us, and still gentler acceptance of the fact that much we see in others is still out of our own reach. The prayer of the growing spirit should be free, humble, simple; full of confidence and full of initiative too. The mystics constantly tell us, that the goal of this prayer and of the hidden life which shall itself become more and more of a prayer, is union with God. We meet this phrase often: far too often, for we lose the wholesome sense of its awfulness. What does union with God mean? Not a nice feeling which we enjoy in devout moments. This may or may not be a by-product of union with God; probably not. It can never be its substance. Union with God means such an entire self-giving to the Divine Charity, such identification with its interests, that the whole of our human nature is transformed in God, irradiated by His absolute light, His sanctifying grace. Thus it is woven up into the organ of His creative activity, His redeeming purpose; conformed to the pattern of Christ, heart, soul, mind and strength. Each time this happens, it means that one more creature has achieved its destiny; and each soul in whom the life of the Spirit is born, sets out towards that goal.

If men and women want to know what this means in terms of human nature and human experience, one sovereign way is offered them; the contemplation of Christ's life. There we see that we are not to grow in wisdom and stature for our own sakes, in order to achieve what is really a self-interested spirituality. The growth is for a reason that points beyond ourselves: in order that the teaching, healing, life-changing power of the Divine Charity may possess us, and work through us.

*The School of Charity*, pp. 48–9

# Co-operation with God

The servants of God cannot do their best unless they are their best; and therefore self-deepening and self-improvement are the very heart of their job. [And] being one's best, for Christians, depends on and requires the active co-operation and close union of God's grace and our will: docility and effort both at once. Out of *your* struggles and temptations, *your* generous acts of utter self-abandonment to the purposes of God – out of all these different kinds of purification taken together, something has to be made, with which the Holy Spirit can do His work on other souls. Because that is the way in which He does do His work on other souls.

In other words: Our deepest life consists in a willed correspondence with the world of Spirit, and this willed correspondence, which is prayer, is destined to fulfil itself along two main channels; in love towards God and in love towards humanity – two loves which at last and at their highest become one love. Sooner or later, in varying degrees, the power and redeeming energy of God will be manifested through those who thus reach out in desire, first towards Him and then towards other souls. And we, living and growing personalities, are required to become ever more and more spiritualized, ever more and more persuasive, more and more deeply real; in order that we may fulfil this Divine purpose.

This is not mere pious fluff. This is a terribly practical job; the only way in which we can contribute to the bringing in of the Kingdom of God. Theological restatement will not do it. Holiness *will* do it.

*Concerning the Inner Life*, pp. 58–9

# Prayer and Holiness

Creation is change, and change is often painful and mysterious to us. Spiritual creation means a series of changes, which at last produce Holiness, God's aim for men and women.

'O support me,' says Newman, 'as I proceed in this great, awful, happy change, with the grace of Thy unchangeableness. My unchangeableness, here below, is perseverance in changing.' The inner life consists in an enduring of this deep transforming process. The chief object of prayer is to help it on: not merely for our own soul's sake, but for a reason which lifts the devotional life above all pettiness – because this is part of the great creative action which is lifting up humanity to the supernatural order, turning the flour and water of our common nature into the living Bread of Eternal Life. So, the first movement of our prayer must surely be a self-giving to this total purpose, whatever discipline and suffering it may involve for us.

It is a part of the great virtue of self-abandonment, to acknowledge the plain fact that God knows the recipe He is working from and the result He wants to obtain, and we do not. Some need the flame, and respond to its quick action. Others, like the cracknel, come to perfection by moving at a steady pace through the long dark oven which makes a perfect biscuit from a dab of paste. A generous acceptance of his ceaseless creative process, as the thing that matters most in human life, and a willingness to be transformed in whatever way is wanted and at whatever cost, unselfs the inner life, and makes it from the beginning accessible to the searching and delicate action of God; working in ways of which we know nothing, entering and controlling every action, and using every creature, its efforts, sufferings and sacrifices, for the accomplishment of His hidden design.

*The School of Charity*, pp. 19–20

# Prayer and Patience

We often feel that we ought to get on quickly, reach a new stage of knowledge or prayer, like spiritual may-flies. But Christ's short earthly life is divided into thirty years for growth and two and a half for action. The pause, the hush, the hiddenness, which intervenes between the Birth and the Ministry, is part of the divine method, and an earnest of the greatness of that which is to come. Only when that quiet growth has reached the right state is there a revelation of God's purpose, and the stress and discipline of a crucial choice. It is much the same with us in the life of prayer. The Spirit fills us as we grow and make room. To contemplate the life of Christ, said St Augustine, 'cures inflation, and nourishes humility.' We see in Him the gradual action of God, subdued to the material on which it works, and fostering and sanctifying growth – that holy secret process.

All gardeners know the importance of good root development before we force the leaves and flowers. So our life in God should be deeply rooted and grounded before we presume to expect to produce flowers and fruits; otherwise we risk shooting up into one of those lanky plants which can never do without a stick. We are constantly beset by the notion that we ought to perceive ourselves springing up quickly, like the seed on stony ground; show striking signs of spiritual growth. But perhaps we are only required to go on quietly, making root, growing nice and bushy; docile to the great slow rhythm of life. When we see no startling marks of our own religious progress or our usefulness to God, it is well to remember the baby in the stable and the little boy in the streets of Nazareth. The very life was there present, which was to change the whole history of the human race; the rescuing action of God. At that stage there was not much to show for it; yet there is perfect continuity between the stable and the Easter garden, and the thread that unites them is the hidden Will of God. The childish prayer of Nazareth was the right preparation for the awful prayer of the Cross.

*The School of Charity*, pp. 47–8

# Prayer and Action (1)

Prayer is our nearest approach to absolute action; it means the closest association of which any soul is at any time capable with the living and everywhere present God who is the true initiator of all that we really do. Progress in it is really a progressive surrender of the conditioned creature to that unconditioned yet richly personal Reality, who is the only source, teacher and object of prayer. Its whole wonder and mystery abide in this: that here, our tiny souls are being invited and incited to communion with God, the Eternal Spirit of the Universe.

Hence the self that fully gives its mind and will to prayer at once moves out actually if not consciously to the border between the natural and supernatural worlds, and changes its relation to both. So whether a prayer seems to him who prays to be introversive or out-flying, contemplative or intercessory in type, does not perhaps matter very much; since it is, in essence, a non-spatial activity, expressed in such particular forms or ways as lie within the limited grasp and understanding of each soul. It may find its embodiment in gesture, action, liturgic or spontaneous words. The Catholic procession, the Quaker silence, the Methodist prayer-meeting, the Salvationist's tambourine, can all justify themselves in the presence of the one God. Prayer may equally find its fulfilment in a special use of rhythm and cadence, in phrases which direct and support attention and desire, or in a state of soul apparently unrelated to the centres of speech; the profoundly absorbed and satisfying prayer of quiet or of union, as described by the mystics. Whatever its kind or degree, it means for the praying soul an interweaving in experience – not necessarily in intellectual realization – of two already present orders; and the mystics are surely right when they insist that its essence is a resort of the creature to that metaphysical 'ground of the soul', where every spirit inheres in God and already in a measure partakes of eternal life, since 'God, the ground of the soul, and grace go together.'

*Man and the Supernatural*, pp. 196–8

# Prayer and Action (2)

Living as we mostly do within the narrow bounds of a sense-conditioned consciousness, it is always good to remind ourselves first that this human capacity for spiritual action does exist; and next that its real nature and extent are still largely unknown to us. As the physical forces on which life depends are hidden, and known to us not in their essence but in their effect; so the life of the Spirit far exceeds in its factualness that which it seems to us to be. Its dark and powerful rays, its enlightening, quickening and attractive forces, permeate the little fragile creature; healing and supporting, inciting and preventing, at every point and in every way. This truth should surely keep us in humility as regards our tiny and limited religious apprehensions; and in delighted confidence, as regards the unmeasured possibilities opened up to us in prayer. It is at once bracing and humbling, thus to remember our relation to the unsearchable Source of that mysterious sunshine of which we sometimes feel a little, that boundless generous air which we take as it were for granted and almost unconsciously breathe. There, surrounding, bathing and transfusing us, but in its reality infinitely transcending us, is that unmeasured and living world with its powers, its beneficent influences; and here are we, capable of a certain communion with it, of action through and within it. The whole *rationale* of prayer is bound up in the belief that such action is possible, and transcends in power and obligation its mere outward or physical expression. Prayer in its fullness commits us to the belief that the eternal world of Spirit is the world of power; and that we are not fully active until we are contemplative too.

*Man and the Supernatural*, pp. 202–3

# Prayer and Action (3)

[What] the saints show us again and again in the various beauty of their lives – is that we are not required to go outside the frame of normal experience in order to fulfil the creative design of God for souls. There is no place and no career which lies outside Eternity, and cannot incarnate something of the Eternal Charity. What was done in the carpenter's shop can be done in the engineer's shop too. 'Perfect God and perfect Man' is a formula which endorses our ordinary human life, even in its most forbidding phases, as fully adequate to the demands of spiritual life; so long as that human life really has one Lord. It matters little that the stable gives way before the garage, the temple before the church, or that hydroplanes alight on the Sea of Galilee.

This is surely an important truth for us. It shows that there need be no separation, no forced option between our life of action and our life of prayer. In the saints, the action and the prayer are mixed together, and make something quite concrete. 'The mirage shall become a pool!' says Isaiah. The lovely glowing dream seen in our meditations becomes a genuine reality, a source of living water for the thirsty, when we find ourselves in the disconcerting presence of a saint. There are plenty of spiritual systems which show us the beautiful mirage. Only in Christianity does it become a pool, a reservoir of living water to refresh our thirsty world.

*The School of Charity*, pp. 33–4

# Prayer and Freedom

Prayer enters deeply into history, and is explicated in traditional and historic ways; and yet it transcends history. It affects our physical and mental status, transforms to its purpose and fills with new ardour the homely symbols of our emotional life, takes colour from the senses and gives a deepened significance to their reports; yet alone moves freely in the regions beyond sense. It is *with God*, and therefore omnipresent. The praying soul, the man who is really 'in the Spirit', is experiencing human freedom in its most intense form, and realizing its latent capacity for spiritual action . . .

Therefore a primary duty among the great human duties – perhaps the greatest of all – is willed and faithful correspondence with that Eternal World, and action within it: a correspondence and an action which gradually spread from their focus in deliberate devotional acts, till they include and transfuse the whole of life. The capital possibility offered to us in prayer – taking this word now in its most general sense – is that we can genuinely achieve this: and that our small and derivative spirits, by such humble willed communion with the very Source of their being and power, can grow and expand into tools of the creative love and power. Within the atmosphere of prayer, virtual and actual – but only within that atmosphere – we can expand from narrow individualities into personalities capable of being fully used on supernatural levels for supernatural work. This is of course the state of holiness; and holiness, the achievement of a creative supernatural personality capable of furthering the Divine action within life, is the true assigned end of the faithfully pursued and completely developed individual life of prayer.

*Man and the Supernatural*, pp. 201–3

# The Fruits of the Spirit

The reality, the living quality of our prayer, our communion with God, can best be tested by the gradual growth in us of these fruits of Divine Love. They are real fruits and therefore they grow by their inherent vitality, at their own pace, hardly observed till they are ripe. They are not something we can model with deliberate effort in spiritual plasticine. Perhaps you think you have only produced a few small green apples – wait patiently till the sunshine of God brings them to maturity.

'The fruit of the Spirit,' says St Paul, 'is Love, Joy, Peace, Long-suffering, Gentleness, Goodness, Faithfulness, Meekness, Temperance' – all the things the world most needs. A clear issue, is it not? To discover the health and reality of our life of prayer, we need not analyse it or fuss about it. But we must consider whether it tends, or does not tend, to produce just these fruits, because they are the necessary results of the action of God in the soul. These are the fruits of human nature when it has opened itself to the action of the Eternal Love: what the 'new creature in Christ' (which if we are really Christians, we are all in the process of becoming) is to be like. So they are very good subjects for meditation. A good gardener always has an idea of what he is trying to grow; without vision even a cabbage patch will perish.

*The Fruits of the Spirit*, pp. 5–6

# Faith, Hope and Charity

By Faith we mean the lifting up into God of our human power of understanding the world; by Hope, the state in which our whole mental content, our 'apperceiving mass' is penetrated and transmuted by our confident expectation of Him; by Charity, that glowing friendship between Creator and created, which merges our will into His will. Thus all three are forms of one thirst for ultimate Being, the drive of personality towards God; and at their fullness merge into one act or state, which lifts the soul up and out beyond itself and the interests of its own small house to a certain loving participation in Eternal Life.

For real prayer is simply the expression and the experience of Faith, Hope and Charity; each penetrating and enhancing the other, and merging to form in us that state of energetic and loving surrender, in which our spirits have according to their measure communion with the Spirit of God.

*The House of the Soul*, pp. 110–11

# THE STAGES OF PRAYER

*Evelyn had little to say on* technique *in prayer. She did not offer a detailed, practical guide to teaching yourself to pray. She could not, for she truly believed that 'God is the true initiator of all that we really do',[1] therefore prayer is not something we do ourselves.*

*Of course Evelyn recognized that there were problems in praying – that it is a 'difficult art'; and that the greatest authorities on the subject (e.g. St Teresa) were dangerous in the hands of beginners and probably incomprehensible to many. Evelyn was used to dealing with well-meaning but over-ambitious souls who were trying too hard to make 'progress'. 'I wish you could forget . . . that this word [progress] exists!', she told Z. A., who was, she said, 'too anxious, too impatient.'[2]*

*She constantly advised against checking spiritual pulses and getting 'the bulb out of the dark to see how it is getting on!'[3] 'It is quite impossible', she maintained, 'for any of us to measure ourselves and estimate our progress.'[4]*

*So why, then, did she write an article on the states of prayer? Surely any endeavour to define a variety of types of prayer and place them in a fixed order would only serve as an inducement to readers to plot their 'progress'? As we will see, she is careful to guard against this possibility.*

*Evelyn indicates that she is writing for those who are reasonably proficient or involved in helping others. Clear guidelines are given. She recognized that we need to know there is more than one way of praying, for then 'there is always some way of turning to God which is within our reach, however distracted or weary we may be'.[5]*

*Even so, she deliberately did* not *deal with the higher stages of prayer, lest she encourage the over-ambitious, and those looking for 'experiences' rather than seeking God where he could best be found – in their daily lives. 'The ultimate object of all prayer is greater efficiency for God, not the limp self-abandonment of quietism.'[6]*

*And so we find no advice about breathing techniques, special postures, short cuts or 'spiritual tricks'. Silence, surrender, perseverance, co-operation, penitence, a 'devout intent', the desire to* pray – these are what lead to the development of the 'simple, natural, unforced character of real intercourse with God'.[7]

Patience and trust are also essential, for 'God feeds and leads the soul very gently. Growth is gradual',[8] and God is the initiator.

Finally, humility 'is the one grace that gives wings to the simplest prayer'.[9] If God wants us to sit at the foot of the ladder of love, then that is our place until he tells us to 'go up higher'.

1. Evelyn Underhill, *Man and the Supernatural*, p. 196.
2. Charles Williams (ed.), *The Letters of Evelyn Underhill*, p. 187.
3. *ibid.* p. 169.
4. *ibid.* p. 187.
5. Evelyn Underhill, *Collected Papers*, p. 50.
6. *ibid.* p. 46.
7. *ibid.* p. 38.
8. *ibid.* p. 39.
9. *ibid.* p. 50.

# The Need for Guidance

I wish to consider our own prayerful activities in the light of the certain fact that there *are* quite definite and different grades and sorts of prayer, which do appear to be the normal expressions of different grades and sorts of souls at various periods of their growth. It seems to me well that all those truly in earnest about the practice of the inner life, and especially those trying to help other souls, should realize and study this; not in order that we may always be feeling our own devotional pulses – for nothing is worse than that – but in order that we may learn to deal wisely with our own souls, and better understand the problems of those who come to us for help.

In prayer, we open up our souls to the Divine energy and grace perpetually beating in on us; and receive that energy and grace, in order that it may be transmuted by our living zest into work – may cleanse, invigorate and slowly change us. It is therefore of primary importance to all Christians to know how best to set up and maintain the contacts of prayer. This is a difficult art – we should bring intelligence as well as love to bear on it. It is all very well to say that you will find it all in St Teresa. For persons of mature experience, the writings of St Teresa are the most exact of guides; but they are guides to the mountains, and can be misunderstood by the novice, or even lead into danger those who are hasty and untrained. Emotional temperaments, too, can find in such books an excuse for revelling in mere devotionalism; and this is contrary to the true ethos of Christian spirituality. Christian spirituality seeks union with God in order that we may better serve the purposes of His will; and one of the ways in which this is done is by the expansion of the prayerful consciousness. Anything, therefore, which we can find out about this is a true extension of our knowledge of the Kingdom of Heaven.

'The Degrees of Prayer', from *Collected Papers*, pp. 36–7

# The Need for Simplicity

The first thing that occurs to us is, that all the machinery of prayer has but one very simple object – our loving intercourse with God – and that all progress in it can be described as an increased closeness in the intercourse and an increased perfection in the love. The varieties and degrees of the machinery have in themselves no intrinsic importance, except in so far as they contribute to this. We study them, as we study the normal development of bodily or mental activity, because we find, in practice, that they occur; and it is better and more healthy to know this, than to be baffled and puzzled when, for instance, we find ourselves for the first time plunged in the prayer of simplicity, and unable to make use of our ordinary forms. But, in considering our own prayer, it is of little importance to ask ourselves whether we have attained this or that degree, but of great importance to ask ourselves what is the condition and attitude of our souls in the degree which we find ourselves to be practising – whether this prayer is truly humbling, bracing, and vivifying us, or merely inducing a state of emotional languor or spiritual strain. All the greatest masters of prayer bring home to us the simple, natural, unforced character of real intercourse with God. They say again and again that prayer is nothing else but a devout intent directed towards Him; and this intent expresses itself in various ways. The beginner must be shown these ways, and often be helped to use them; but in the mature man or woman of prayer their exercise is free and spontaneous. Perhaps there is no other department of the spiritual life in which St Augustine's great saying, 'Love, and do what you like,' becomes more completely true.

'The Degrees of Prayer', from *Collected Papers*, pp. 37–8

# Real Inner Silence

The soul's real progress is not towards some mysterious, abnormal and trance-like condition; but rather towards the unspoilt, trustful, unsophisticated apprehension of the little child. This is what matters; not the special degree in which it is experienced. Thus a badly held, distracted attempt at the prayer of simplicity, involving tension and effort, and therefore self-consciousness, has far less spiritual content than an unforced, humble and natural vocal prayer. In prayer, will and grace co-operate. Neither a limp abandonment to the supposed direction of the Spirit, nor a vigorous determination to wrestle with God, on our own account, will do for it. Our willed self-donation conditions the reception of grace: grace conditions the power of the prayerful will. Hence it is useless to endeavour by willed struggle, or by obeying the rules in ascetic manuals, to reach a level of prayer to which we are not yet impelled by grace. We cannot by stretching ourselves add an inch to our stature: the result will be strain, not growth. All this means that we should be very chary of taking at face value the advice given in little books about 'going into the silence' and so on: and should never treat this advice as though it were applicable to every soul at every time. Real inward silence is not achieved by any deliberate spiritual trick. It develops naturally; and most often from the full exercise of mental prayer, which is in its turn the child of properly practised vocal prayer. Therefore I think that no one ought to set to work to practise such inward silence until they feel a strong impulse so to do. If we try such artificial methods, we probably drift into a mere quietistic reverie; and such reverie, though pleasant, has nothing in common with real contemplative prayer.

'The Degrees of Prayer', from *Collected Papers*, pp. 38–9

# Growth is Gradual

We shall do best if we enter on the study of the degrees of prayer safeguarded by this principle: that whilst keeping in mind the highest ideal of attainment, we are never to struggle for a degree or condition of fervour in which we do not naturally find ourselves. People are often encouraged to do this by indiscriminate reading of ascetic and mystical literature, a practice to which real dangers are attached. They browse among descriptions and counsels intended only for advanced souls, and struggle to produce states of consciousness far beyond their power. These states will arise within us naturally and simply, only when and if we are ready for them. In all normal cases, God feeds and leads the soul very gently. Growth is gradual. The many adjustments necessary to the full establishment of the prayerful consciousness take time; and often its advance is checked by periods of dullness, fatigue and incapacity which are explicable by psychology, and must be borne with patience as instruments of our purification. All the great masters of prayer refer to them, and insist, too, that humble surrender, not constant fervour, is the best index of the soul's good-will. Thus Walter Hilton says: 'When thou disposest thee to think of God, if thy heart be dull and dark, and feels neither wit nor savour not devotion for to think, but only a bare desire and a weak will that thou wouldst think of God, but thou canst not – then I hope it is good to thee that thou strive not much with thyself, as if thou wouldst by thine own might overcome thyself.' Here Hilton shows himself to be intuitively aware of that which psychologists now call the law of Reversed Effort – the fact that such desperate striving with ourselves merely frustrates its own end, and increases our baffled sense of helplessness. And again, to the soul dissatisfied with its ordinary prayers and hankering after contemplation, he says: 'Press not too much thereafter, as if thou wert abiding or gaping after some strange stirring or some wonderful feeling other than thou hast had.' And another old English mystic tells us not to be like 'greedy greyhounds' snatching at God's gifts, but to come gently and willingly to His outstretched hand and take what He gives us.

'The Degrees of Prayer', from *Collected Papers*, pp. 39–40

# Vocal Prayer

I propose now to make five divisions: and these are – Vocal Prayer, Meditation, the Prayer of Immediate Acts, the Prayer of Simplicity, the Prayer of Quiet. Beyond these are the higher degrees of contemplation, which are outside our present scope.

First, then, comes Vocal Prayer. We all know what this is; but we do not always remember, in our eagerness for something more spiritual, that apart from its devotional aspect its educative value for the soul that uses it is greater than is sometimes supposed. In vocal prayer we speak, not only to God, but also to ourselves. We are filling our minds with acts of love, praise, humility and penitence, which will serve us well in times when the power of mental prayer seems to fail us and the use of these formulas becomes the only way of turning to God left within our reach. Moreover, psychology insists that the spoken word has more suggestive power, is more likely to reach and modify our deeper psychic levels, than any inarticulate thought; for the centres of speech are closely connected with the heart of our mental life. Therefore those who value the articulate recitation of a daily office, the use of litanies and psalms, are keeping closer to the facts of existence than those who only talk generally of remaining in a state of prayer. I feel sure that some vocal prayer should enter into the daily rule even of the most contemplative soul. It gives shape and discipline to our devotions, and keeps us in touch with the great traditions of the Church. Moreover, such vocal prayers, if we choose them well, have the evocative quality of poetry: they rouse the dormant spiritual sense, and bring us into the presence of God. 'Oft it falls,' says Hilton, 'that praying with thy mouth gets and keeps fervour of devotion, and if a man cease from saying, devotion vanishes away.'

'The Degrees of Prayer', from *Collected Papers*, pp. 41–2

# Meditation (1)

As the life of prayer begins to exert its full power, such vocal prayers will gradually but steadily become slower and more pondered. The soul finds in their phrases more and more significance, makes of these phrases special applications, and is led on by them to petitions and aspirations of its own. This means that it is drawing near to the next stage, that of meditation. Meditation is a word which covers a considerable range of devotional states. It is perhaps most simply defined as thinking in the Presence of God. And since our ordinary thoughts are scattered, seldom poised for long on one point, but evoked and influenced by a multitude of external things, real meditation requires as its preliminary what ascetic writers call recollection – a deliberate gathering of ourselves together, a retreat into our own souls. This is more easily done by a simple exercise of the imagination, a gentle turning to God, than by those ferocious efforts towards concentrating which some manuals advise, and which often end by concentrating attention on the concentration itself. There is no virtue in any one method, except in so far as it succeeds; and different methods succeed with different souls. For some, the slow reading of a passage in the Bible or the *Imitation* leads directly to a state of prayer: for others, a quiet dwelling on one of God's attributes is a gateway to adoration. Articulate speech is now left aside, but the ceaseless stream of inward discourse may persist, and become a secret conversation with God; while others will be led to consideration, a quiet ruminating on spiritual things. As to Three-point Meditations and so on, it is perhaps enough if we keep in mind that every real meditation, however short, natural and artless, does involve three points: for our mind, will and feelings are all exercised in it. We think in some way of the subject of our meditation. We feel the emotion, whether of love, penitence or joy, which it suggests to us. And finally, the aim of all meditative prayer is a resolution, or a renewal of our surrender to God: and this is an act of the will.

'The Degrees of Prayer', from *Collected Papers*, pp. 42–4

# The Prayer of Immediate Acts

The transition from meditation to immediate acts takes place only in those souls which have some tendency to contemplation; not perhaps much, but still an aptitude seeking expression. By them it is commonly felt as a decreasing inclination to reason or discourse in prayer, and an increasing inclination to simple, spontaneous expressions of love and penitence. It is true that the praying self does think; but not with the same method and completeness as before. It now dwells more and more on the affections; on acts of love and adoration, meek aspirations to God, expressed in short phrases which may seem banal enough when we read them in books of devotion, but become charged, for the soul in this degree, with the most intense significance. We remember the favourite aspiration of St Francis: 'My God, my God, what art Thou and what am I?' Such aspirations, formed from memories of past reading and prayers, rise spontaneously into consciousness as the prayer proceeds; and those whose minds are richly stored with Scripture phrases and liturgic forms will seldom be at a loss for them. They are, however, only the expression of the act. 'Press thou towards God with the sharp dart of thy longing love,' says the author of *The Cloud of Unknowing* in his directions for this prayer, 'and take no thought for words.' Intuition here begins to take the place of logical considerations; and, as psychologists would say, affective thought as well as rational thought is taken up into the life of prayer, which now overflows its first boundaries and invades wider and wider regions of the self.

'The Degrees of Prayer', from *Collected Papers*, pp. 44–5

# The Prayer of Simplicity

As this degree matures in those to whom it is appropriate, the 'immediate acts' of the heart decrease and will grow simpler and rarer. There is often a marked distaste and inability for meditation. There are pauses, periods of deep silence, hushed communion which the soul feels to be more and more fruitful. Here we are at the threshold of that progressive absorption which leads to the true contemplative state. Gradually one act of will, affection or aspiration comes more and more to dominate the whole prayer, say of half an hour's duration or more: and is used merely to true up that state of attention which is the very heart of prayer. When this condition is established, the soul has reached the degree which is sometimes called the prayer of simplicity, and sometimes that of response, simple attention or active contemplation. It is thrown open with great love and desire to God, but in so simple a way that it cannot analyse its own experience. Its whole impulse is to wait on Him rather than to speak to Him. It was in the effort to describe the apprehensions of this degree that the author of *The Cloud of Unknowing* said, 'God may well be loved, but not thought. Therefore I will leave all I can think and take to my love that which I cannot think.' Nevertheless I am sure it is a mistake to imagine that such prayer can be well developed and preserved, unless a certain care be given to its mental preparation. It is far better to enter it with *some* idea or disposition in the mind, some special thought of God, some distinct orientation of the will, than in the state of vague blankness characteristic of quietism; for this will merely encourage distraction and religious day-dreams, and may even bring about a sort of self-hypnotization. The ultimate object of all prayer is greater efficiency for God, not the limp self-abandonment of quietism.

'The Degrees of Prayer', from *Collected Papers*, pp. 45–6

# The Night of the Senses

The real Prayer of Quiet, is wholly involuntary. None can produce it of themselves; and it seems always to come as a distinct and irresistible experience from without. In technical terms, it is 'infused' or the work of grace. In this real quiet, which may come suddenly upon the soul in the course of its ordinary prayer, it is not merely drawn towards a simple and imageless attention to God and aspiration towards Him. It is more or less intensely aware of His Presence. Here, in fact, we have the first faint emergence of the mystical consciousness, in stillness and humility receiving the obscure impression of the Divine. In the prayer of simplicity and aspiration, the deeps of the unconscious are opened up to God; and that this is veritably done in these degrees is proved by their effect on the impulsive sources of conduct. But in the quiet, and the simple union which is the full development of quiet, this apprehension overflows into consciousness; and this is something which the self cannot effect by the exercise of will.

Sometimes the establishment of this new degree comes by way of a painful inward struggle and aridity; what St John of the Cross has described as 'the night of the senses' – a period of distress and obscurity in which it seems to the soul that it is losing all it had gained of the life of prayer. This is more especially felt by people who have real contemplative aptitude, and whom this type of spirituality is destined in the end to dominate. It meets and must conquer many resistances in their active minds, must cut for itself new paths; and this may involve tension and suffering and the apparent withdrawal of the ordinary power of prayer. Here is a point at which skilled and sympathetic guidance is of special service to the soul, which is often bewildered and disheartened by its own experience, its strange sense of dimness and incapacity. Others, whose natural level is, and may always remain, the prayer of aspiration or of simplicity, may find themselves plunged in the quiet from time to time; and will obtain from this experience a refreshment, power and absolute certitude which the other degrees of prayer cannot give.

'The Degrees of Prayer', from *Collected Papers*, pp. 47–9

# The Ladder of Love

The use of the higher degrees of prayer does not and should not ever mean the total abandonment of the lower degrees. To suppose this is the fundamental error of quietism. The healthiness of our spiritual life, like that of our mental life, depends to a great extent on its suppleness, and on the variety which we are able to impart to it. We should never, therefore, be afraid of such variety, or suppose we are losing ground if we find ourselves again using discursive prayer or formal acts after practising the higher degrees. The mystics are insistent on this point. Thus St John of the Cross says, that when the soul is not in the prayer of simplicity it 'ought to avail itself in all its exercises of the help of good thoughts and meditations, according to what brings it the greatest spiritual profit.' And St Teresa still more strongly – 'Since God has given the powers of the soul in order that we may use them, and the work of each has its reward, instead of trying to imprison them by a sort of enchantment let them freely perform their ordinary office, until it pleases God to raise them to a higher state.'

It is therefore best to be ready to go up and down the ladder of love: sometimes speaking and sometimes listening, sometimes thinking and sometimes resting in the communion which is beyond thought and speech. A quiet and meek retreat to a lower degree of prayer, which one *can* do, is worth far more than the anxious struggle to tune oneself up to a degree which (anyhow for the moment) one cannot do. Self-will in prayer is a subtle temptation, known to most religious people. But there is always some way of turning to God which is within our reach, however distracted or weary we may be: and as a general rule, it is surely better to begin there, quite simply, though the crudity and childishness of our level of feeling and expression may deal a smart blow at our self-respect. Constituted as we are, it is inevitable that our spiritual aptitude should fluctuate, as does the rest of our plastic and unstable psychic life. This limitation ought not to depress us, but it ought to keep us in humility; and humility is the one grace which gives wings to the simplest prayer.

'The Degrees of Prayer', from *Collected Papers*, pp. 49–50

# PRAYER AND BELIEF

As we observed in the chapters on prayer and the stages of prayer, Evelyn Underhill did not focus on prayer techniques, or offer a practical guide to praying with the minimum of pain and effort.

Yet there is in her prolific writings reference to a 'road-book', a 'map', a 'hand-list of the soul's essential requirements'.[1] It is a disclosure, at first strange and puzzling, which 'feeds, enlightens and supports us when we dare to take up the life that it reveals'.[2] It is 'our list of spiritual truths to which our inner life must be conformed.'[3]

The creed is the unequivocal affirmation of the reality of God, and the undeniable witness to the priority of God. In the following extracts from The School of Charity – a book which was originally presented as a retreat – we see clearly that, for Evelyn, prayer is the unequivocal affirmation of the reality of God and the undeniable witness to the priority of God.

As in the chapters on saints and mystics and the spiritual life and mysticism, we find that Evelyn never divorces the spiritual life from the practicalities of the everyday world: indeed, the Creed tests 'our vague, dilute, self-occupied spirituality' by its 'superb Vision of Reality'.[4]

Nor is there any conflict between prayer and belief. 'Lex credendi, lex orandi',[5] she quotes with conviction.

As always, Evelyn expresses these profound truths in simple, earthy, homely language. The first three extracts are a good example of this, and warn against the dangers of not caring for our spiritual store-houses and not keeping our 'religious equipment' in good order. The analogy is simple: when we go on a journey, we may take bottles and tins of food with us, but if we can't read the labels and forget to take a tin-opener, we could still starve to death!

The Creed is no 'mere academic document, no mere list of "dogmas" ';[6] it is the revelation of divine love, of the Divine Charity. Like the Eucharist, it feeds us. Will we accept the invitation to eat?

1. Evelyn Underhill, *The School of Charity*, p. 4.
2. *ibid.* p. 5.
3. *ibid.* p. 10.
4. *ibid.* p. 6.
5. *ibid.* p. 6.
6. *ibid.* p. 5.

# The Risk of Spiritual Starvation

Everyone who is engaged on a great undertaking, depending on many factors for its success, knows how important it is to have a periodical stocktaking. Whether we are responsible for a business, an institution, a voyage, or an exploration – even for the well-being of a household – it is sometimes essential to call a halt; examine our stores and our equipment, be sure that all necessaries are there and in good order, and that we understand the way in which they should be used. It is no good to have tins without tin openers, bottles of which the contents have evaporated, labels written in an unknown language, or mysterious packages of which we do not know the use. Now the living-out of the spiritual life, the inner life of the Christian – the secret correspondence of his soul with God – is from one point of view a great business. It was well called 'the business of all businesses' by St Bernard; for it is no mere addition to Christianity, but its very essence, the source of its vitality and power. From another point of view it is a great journey; a bit-by-bit progress, over roads that are often difficult and in weather that is sometimes pretty bad, from 'this world to that which is to come.' Whichever way we look at it, an intelligent and respectful attitude to our equipment – seeing that it is all there, accessible and in good condition, and making sure that we know the real use of each item – is essential to success. It is only too easy to be deluded by the modern craving for pace and immediate results, and press on without pausing to examine the quality and character of our supplies, or being sure that we know where we are going and possess the necessary maps. But this means all the disabling miseries of the unmarked route and unbalanced diet; and at last, perhaps, complete loss of bearings and consequent starvation of the soul.

*The School of Charity*, pp. 1–2

# Maintaining Our Religious Equipment

That dreadful situation [spiritual starvation] can easily become our own, if we merely take our religious equipment for granted; do not make sure that it contains food on which we can feed, tins we can open, and that we know what the labels really mean. For the spiritual life cannot be maintained on a diet of suggestive phrases and ideas. Only when we have found within the familiar externals of our religion, those vivid realities which these externals enclose and keep safe, are we using our equipment properly and getting the food we need. We must open the tins, if we are to discover inside them the mysterious nourishment of the soul. Nor have we any right to ask for fresh enlightenment, or a new issue of provisions, until we have fully explored the resources we already possess.

This process is equally necessary for those who are repelled by the externals of religion, and those who are attracted by them. Both need to recognize the difference between the container and the content. Many people spend the whole of their devotional lives sitting by the wayside admiring the pictures on the tins; more are alienated from religion by mistaking this procedure for faith.

*The School of Charity*, pp. 2–3

# Spiritual Stocktaking

Lent is a good moment for spiritual stocktaking; a pause, a retreat from life's busy surface to its solemn deeps. There we can consider our possessions; and discriminate between the necessary stores which have been issued to us, and must be treasured and kept in good order, and the odds and ends which we have accumulated for ourselves. Most of us are inclined to pay considerable attention to the spiritual odds and ends: the air-cushions, tabloids, and vacuum flasks, and various labour-saving devices which we call by such attractive names as our own peace, our own approach, our own experience, and so forth. But we leave the superb and massive standard equipment which is issued to each baptized Christian to look after itself. There are few who cannot benefit by a bit by bit examination of that equipment, a humble return to first principles; for there we find the map and road-block of that spiritual world which is our true environment, all the needed information about the laws which control it, and all essentials for feeding that inner life of which we talk so much and understand so very little.

The Christian creed is a hand-list of the soul's essential requirements: the iron ration of truths, the knowledge of mighty realities, which rightly used is sufficient to feed and safeguard our supernatural life throughout its course.

*The School of Charity*, pp. 3–4

# Our Spiritual Guide

When Christians say the Creed, they say in effect, 'This is what we believe to be the truth about existence; about God and the things of God, and so by implication about our own mysterious lives.' For the whole of life, visible and invisible, is governed by these statements; which come to us from beyond our normal radius, entering the human scene in their penetrating truth and majestic beauty, to show us how to live.

The longer we go on with life, the more mysterious, the more baffling it seems to most of us: and the more deeply we feel the need of being taught how to live. We go muddling on, secretly conscious that we are making a mess of it. Guides come forward to tell us this or that, yet always with an avoidance of the full mystery of our situation, seldom with any real sense of the richness of the material of life: and they all fail to be of much use to us when we come to the bad bits. The surface-indications often mislead us. The tangle of new roads, bordered by important-looking factories and unhappy little trees, the arterial highways leading nowhere, the conflicting demands and directions which reach us from every side, only make our confusions worse. And at last we realize that only the Author of human life can teach us how to live human life, because He alone sees it in its eternal significance: and He does this by a disclosure that at first may seem strange and puzzling, but grows in beauty and meaning as we gaze at it, and which feeds, enlightens and supports us when we dare to take up the life that it reveals.

*The School of Charity*, pp. 4–5

# The Hand-List of Deep Truths

'Lord,' said St Thomas Aquinas, 'set my life in order; making me to know what I ought to do and do it in the way that I should.' The civilized world seems now to have reached the point at which only this prayer can save it; and the answer is already given us in the Christian creed. We talk much of reconstruction; but no one has yet dared to take the Christian's profound beliefs about Reality as the basis of a reconditioned world. We treat them as dwellers in the plain treat the mountains. We lift up our eyes to their solemn beauty with respect; but refuse to acknowledge that plain and mountain are part of the same world. Yet the Creed is no mere academic document, no mere list of 'dogmas.' It is an account of that which *is*; and every word it contains has a meaning at once universal, practical, and spiritual within the particular experience of each soul. It irradiates and harmonizes every level of our life, not one alone. All great spiritual literature does this to some extent; but the Creed, the condensed hand-list of those deep truths from which spiritual literature is built up, does it supremely.

*The School of Charity, p. 5*

# Prayer and Belief

The spiritual life is a stern choice. It is not a consoling retreat from the difficulties of existence; but an invitation to enter fully into that difficult existence, and there apply the Charity of God and bear the cost. Till we accept this truth, religion is full of puzzles for us, and its practices often unmeaning: for we do not know what it is all about. So there are few things more bracing and enlightening than a deliberate resort to these superb statements about God, the world and the soul; testing by them our attitude to those realities, and the quality and vigour of our interior life with God. For every one of them has a direct bearing on that interior life. *Lex credendi, lex orandi.* Our prayer and belief should fit like hand and glove; they are the inside and outside of one single correspondence with God. Since the life of prayer consists in an ever-deepening communion with a Reality beyond ourselves, which is truly there, and touches, calls, attracts us, what we believe about that Reality will rule our relation to it. We do not approach a friend and a machine in the same way. We make the first and greatest of our mistakes in religion when we begin with ourselves, our petty feelings and needs, ideas and capacities. The Creed sweeps us up past all this to GOD, the objective Fact, and His mysterious self-giving to us. It sets first Eternity and then History before us, as the things that truly matter in religion; and shows us a humble and adoring delight in God as the first duty of the believing soul. So there can hardly be a better inward discipline than the deliberate testing of our vague, dilute, self-occupied spirituality by this superb vision of Reality.

*The School of Charity,* p. 6

# God First

Christian prayer to God must harmonize with Christian belief about God: and quickly loses humility and sanity if it gets away from that great law. We pray first because we believe something; perhaps at that stage a very crude or vague something. And with the deepening of prayer, its patient cultivation, there comes – perhaps slowly, perhaps suddenly – the enrichment and enlargement of belief, as we enter into a first-hand communion with the Reality who is the object of our faith.

For God, not man, is the first term of religion: and our first step in religion is the acknowledgement that HE IS. All else is the unfolding of those truths about His life and our life, which this fact of facts involves. I believe in One God. We begin there; not with our own needs, desires, feelings, or obligations. Were all these abolished, His independent splendour would remain, as the Truth which gives its meaning to the world. So we begin by stating with humble delight our belief and trust in the most concrete, most rich of all realities – God.

*The School of Charity*, p. 8

# The Reality of Love

Christianity is not a pious reverie, a moral system or a fantasy life; it is a revelation, adapted to our capacity, of the Realities which control life. Those Realities must largely remain unknown to us; limited little creatures that we are. God, as Brother Giles said, is a great mountain of corn from which we, like sparrows, take a grain of wheat: yet even that grain of wheat, which is as much as we can carry away, contains all the essentials of our life. We are to carry it carefully and eat it gratefully: remembering with awe the majesty of the mountain from which it comes.

The first thing this vast sense of God does for us, is to deliver us from the imbecilities of religious self-love and self-assurance; and sink our little souls in the great life of the race, in and upon which this One God in His mysterious independence is always working, whether we notice it or not. When that sense of His unique reality gets dim and stodgy, we must go back and begin there once more; saying with the Psalmist, 'All my fresh springs are in thee.' Man, said Christ, is nourished by every word that proceeds out of the mouth of God. Not the words we expect, or persuade ourselves that we have heard; but those unexpected words He really utters, sometimes by the mouths of the most unsuitable people, sometimes through apparently unspiritual events, sometimes secretly within the soul. Therefore seeking God, and listening to God, is an important part of the business of human life: and this is the essence of prayer. We do something immense, almost unbelievable, when we enter that world of prayer, for then we deliberately move out towards that transcendent Being whom Christianity declares to be the one Reality: a Reality revealed to us in three ways as a Creative Love, a Rescuing Love, and an Indwelling, all-pervading Love, and in each of those three ways claiming and responding to our absolute trust. Prayer is the give-and-take between our little souls and that three-fold Reality.

*The School of Charity,* pp. 8–9

# Infinite Charity

The Creed, our list of the spiritual truths to which our inner life must be conformed, is all about a God who *is* Charity, a Charity that *is* God. It tells us that what we call creation is the never-ceasing action of a self-spending personal love; and all the experiences and acts of religion are simply our small experience of, and response to, the pressure and the call of that same creative Love which rules the stars. 'Behold, Lord, from whence such love proceedeth!' exclaims Thomas à Kempis. It proceeds from the very heart of the universe. For Christians this is the ultimate fact, which must govern the whole conduct of life. We are each created, sought, possessed and maintained by a living Reality that is Charity; truly known by us in and through His free, generous self-giving, and in no other way. The life which we are called upon to manifest in space and time is a living spark of this generous Love. That means that the true demand of religion will never be a demand for correct behaviour or correct belief; but for generosity, as the controlling factor in every relation between ourselves and God and ourselves and others. To look at ourselves and our lives after looking at this great truth is surely enough to bring self-satisfied piety down with a run.

When we look out towards this Love that moves the stars and stirs in the child's heart, and claims our total allegiance and remember that this alone is Reality and we are only real so far as we conform to its demands, we see our human situation from a fresh angle; and perceive that it is both more humble and dependent, and more splendid, than we had dreamed. We are surrounded and penetrated by great spiritual forces, of which we hardly know anything. Yet the outward events of our life cannot be understood, except in their relation to that unseen and intensely living world, the Infinite Charity which penetrates and supports us, the God whom we resist and yet for whom we thirst; who is ever at work, transforming the self-centred desire of the natural creature into the wide-spreading, outpouring love of the citizen of Heaven.

*The School of Charity*, pp. 10–11

# Creative Love

If the Reality of God were small enough to be grasped, it would not be great enough to be adored; and so our holiest privilege would go. 'I count not myself to have grasped; but as one that has been grasped, I press on,' says St Paul. But if all real knowledge here is a humbly delighted knowledge of our own ignorance – if, as the dying artist said, 'The word we shall use most when we get to heaven will be "Oh!" ' – still we can realize something of what it means, to consider our world from this point of view. It means that everything we are given to deal with – including ourselves and our psychological material, however intractable – is the result of the creative action of a personal Love, who despises nothing that He has made. We, then, cannot take the risk of despising anything; and any temptation to do so must be attributed to our ignorance, stupidity or self-love, and recognized as something which distorts our vision of Reality . . .

It is easy to be both sentimental and theological over the more charming and agreeable aspects of Nature. It is very difficult to see its essential holiness beneath disconcerting and hostile appearances with an equable and purified sight; with something of the large, disinterested Charity of God . . .

It is a part of the life of prayer, which is our small attempt to live the life of Charity, to consider the whole creation with a deep and selfless reverence; enter into its wonder, and find in it the mysterious intimations of the Author of Life, maker of all things, Creative Love.

*The School of Charity*, pp. 13, 14, 15

# The Unity of Creation

This truth of the deep unity of creation links us with our lesser relations, and with our greater relations too. It makes us the members of a family, a social order, so rich and various that we can never exhaust its possibilities. 'My little sisters, the birds,' said St Francis. 'I am thy fellow-slave,' said the great angel of the Apocalypse to the seer. We are all serving on one Staff. Our careful pickings and choosings, acceptances and exclusions, likes and dislikes, race prejudice, class prejudice, and all the rest, look rather silly within the glow of that One God, in Whom all live and move and have their being; and the graduated splendour of that creation which is the work of His paternal Love. The Creed shows up human pride for the imbecility it is, and convinces us that realism is the same thing as humility. It insists upon our own utter dependence on the constant, varied, unseen Creative Love; and the narrow span of our understanding of our fellow-creatures – how slight is the material we have for passing judgment on them – because our understanding is no wider than our charity.

*The School of Charity*, pp. 16–17

# True Spirituality

And now we come down to the more painful consideration of all that this demands from us, if our inner and outer life are to match our belief about Reality; and only when this has happened will Christianity conquer the world, harmonizing all things visible and invisible because both are received and loved as the works of One God. There are still far too many Christians in whose souls a sound-proof partition has been erected between the oratory and the kitchen: sometimes between the oratory and the study too. But the creative action of the Spirit penetrates the whole of life, and is felt by us in all sorts of ways. If our idea of that creative action is so restricted that we fail to recognize it working within the homely necessities and opportunities of our visible life, we may well suspect the quality of those invisible experiences to which we like to give spiritual status. 'I found Him very easily among the pots and pans,' said St Teresa. 'The duties of my position take precedence of everything else,' said Elizabeth Leseur; pinned down by those duties to a life which was a constant check on the devotional practices she loved. She recognized the totality of God's creative action, penetrating and controlling the whole web of life.

A genuine inner life must make us more and more sensitive to that moulding power, working upon His creation at every level, not at one alone: and especially to the constant small but expert touches, felt in and through very homely events, upon those half-made, unsteady souls which are each the subject of His detailed care. A real artist will give as much time and trouble to a miniature two inches square, as to the fresco on the Cathedral wall. The true splendour and heart-searching beauty of the Divine Charity is not seen in those cosmic energies which dazzle and confound us; but in the transcendent power which stoops to an intimate and cherishing love, the grave and steadfast Divine action, sometimes painful and sometime gentle, on the small unfinished soul. It is an unflickering belief in this, through times of suffering and conflict, apathy and desperation, in a life filled with prosaic duties and often empty of all sense of God, that the Creed demands of all who are recite it.

*The School of Charity*, pp. 17–18

[ 129 ]

# The Profound Mysteries of God

We are so busy rushing about, so immersed in what we call practical things, that we seldom pause to realize the mysterious truth of our situation: how little we know that really matters, how completely our modern knowledge leaves the deeps of our existence unexplored. We are inclined to leave all that out. But the Creed will not let us leave the mystery out. Christ never left it out. His teaching has a deep recurrent note of awe, a solemn sense of God and the profound mysteries of God: His abrupt creative entrance into every human life, coming to us, touching us, changing us in every crisis, grief, shock, sacrifice, flashing up on life's horizon like lightning just when we had settled down on the natural level, and casting over the landscape a light we had never dreamed of before. The whole teaching of Christ hinges on the deep mystery and awful significance of our existence; and God, as the supreme and ever-present factor in every situation, from the tiniest to the most universal. The span of His understanding goes from the lilies of the field to the most terrible movements of history. He takes in all the darkness and anxiety of our situation, whether social or personal; and within and beyond all, He finds the creative action of God, the one Reality, the one Life, working with a steadfast and unalterable love, sometimes by the direct action of circumstance and sometimes secretly within each soul in prayer. And this creative action, so hidden and so penetrating, is the one thing that matters in human life.

*The School of Charity,* pp. 18–19

# INTERCESSION

Like many people, Evelyn Underhill had difficulty with inter-cession, and not only in the early stages of her life and prayer. As a teenager, she had been openly cynical:

> I don't believe in worrying God with prayers for things we want. If He is omnipotent He knows we want them, and if He isn't, He can't give them to us.[1]

Even in her mid-forties, when writing to her spiritual director, Baron von Hügel, she did not seem to have progressed much beyond this basic level:

> I feel I ought to spend more time in Intercession, and would, if I could feel it did real work. But it is so unreal to me that I forget all about it . . . In general I forget all specific requests – after all, why should one ask for things? To bring one's deepest desires and intentions and moral difficulties into the presence of God and hold them there is, of course, tremen-dously effective, but trying to affect other people's lives in this way seems to me at present to belong more to the realm of idea than to that of concrete fact.[2]

The Baron's response was that she was not yet fully awake to the reality and power of intercession.

Towards the end of her life, when perhaps her memory was even more likely to fail, she confessed to a friend: 'I will try to remember your poor friend, though I'm terribly bad at intercession for indi-viduals.'[3]

Despite these problems, Evelyn did in fact come to a much different and deeper understanding of what intercession was about and what it could effect, and what it meant in relation to God and to others. The mechanical regurgitation of lists of names was no doubt one inescapable and at times necessary part of intercession, but it was not all of it. Intercession without action she believed to be superficial and hypocritical, as she admitted during self-examination in 1923, when, under the heading 'Sloth', she wrote in her journal:

*Don't* make *time for those who need and ask it of me i.e.*
*Jessie. Absurd to pray that Jessie may be comforted if I don't,*
*at my own inconvenience, go and do the comforting.*

*There was for Evelyn, however, a third degree of Intercessory*
*action, in which one could identify so intensely with the subject of*
*the prayer that one became part of their pain. It is a totally* redemptive *view of prayer, inextricably tied to Jesus' suffering and death.*
*Evelyn realized what it meant, and at first baulked at the commit-*
*ment and sacrifice involved.*

> *. . . if I ask myself whether I would face complete spiritual*
> *deprivation for the good of another: e.g. to effect a conver-*
> *sation, I can't do that as yet. So I have not yet got real*
> *Christian love: and the question is, can one intercede genuinely*
> *for anyone, unless ready to pay, if necessary, this price?*[4]

*Eventually Evelyn did meet this challenge, and it took its toll; but*
*she believed it to be the only way for a soul committed to being*
*at one with God.*

*It is this view that the following readings illustrate. It extends*
*also to the corporate dimension of worship, as the number of*
*extracts relating to the intercessions at the Eucharist exemplifies.*
*In the light of the previous chapters on prayer and the stages of*
*prayer, it can be seen that intercession is* not *a separate detached*
*entity, but an essential part of the way we pray and the way we*
*live our lives. Intercessory prayer is far from being a selfish and*
*demanding list of requests. When we truly 'pray from the Cross',*
*the demands may be made of* us!

*Genuine intercession is part of the mystery of sacrifice – and it*
*is costly.*

1. Margaret Cropper, *Evelyn Underhill*, p. 6.
2. *ibid.* p. 91.
3. *ibid.* p. 309.
4. *ibid.* p. 107.

# What is Intercession?

Intercession in its widest and deepest sense is the true business of sanctity; and emerges in some way or degree in all those lives and separate acts which lie in the direction of the Holy. It completes, with Adoration and Communion, the triune life of prayer; and as that life of prayer develops, so do these its three great constituents fuse into one loving act of communion which redeems while it adores and adores while it redeems. But such adoring intercessory action cannot be limited to overtly religious desires and deeds. Since every act and thought of its members affects the whole spiritual society, there is hardly any mental of bodily action which cannot by intention gain or lose intercessory worth.

'All that you do,' says Cardinal Mercier, 'for good or for evil, either benefits or damages the whole society of souls . . . the humblest of you all, by your degree of virtue, and by the work that you are called to do even in the most obscure situation, makes his contribution to the general sanctification of the Church.'

The great surge of cleansing and compelling life we call 'grace' takes and uses these men and women. Lifting them from concentration on the life of nature, it teaches them each in their own way and degree – and often in terms unconnected with theology – the supreme supernatural secret of heroic and redeeming love. As the longing for personal purification and harmony points to a deep need in the human creature, an implicit knowledge of its half-achieved status and spiritual call; so the longing to do in some way this redemptive work – distinctive of all the greatest souls – surely points to a fundamental character of the supernatural life.

Doubtless this redeeming impulse is, and will be, worked out in many ways and at many different levels. The great intercessory action of the whole Supernatural Society, whether it be still within the physical world or beyond (so touchingly acknowledged in the invocation of the Saints), includes all the diverse responses to God, to Supernature, all the aspirations, all the sacrifices made by every type of soul. Both adoration and supplication, both love and renunciation, accepted suffering as well as devoted action, enter into this; and, in religious language, 'prevail with God'.

*Man and the Supernatural*, pp. 257–9

# What Intercession is Not

Intercession is *not* asking God to do difficult things for Mr Jones or Mr. Smith (though as you say sometimes when we are deeply concerned we can't help doing this). It is offering your will and love that God may use them as channels whereby His Spirit of mercy, healing, power, or light, may reach them and achieve *His* purposes in them. We can't do it unless we care, both for God's will and also for 'the whole human family' – but that certainly does not involve knowing all the details about everyone who asks our prayers. God knows the details – we need not. Probably the best kind of intercession is a quite general offering of oneself in union with our Lord – and that is what the total prayer of the Church for the world is. He prays in and through us, lifting up into the supernatural world all souls and causes and setting them before God's face – and it is our privilege to share that 'lifting-up' process. Of course there is and must be a wide variety in the way people pray. For some, 'crude petition' about Tommy's exam, or Aunt Jane's bronchitis is the only sort that is real. We each do what we can, mostly very badly. The point is that we do it with faith and love and offer it to God, who will take from it that act of will and love which alone really matters, and use it where and how He chooses. Perhaps the prayer we make here may find its fulfilment the other side of the world. Perhaps the help we were given in a difficult moment came from a praying soul we never knew! It is all a deep mystery and we should be careful not to lay down hard and fast rules. The variousness with which Grace works is one of the most wonderful things about it. It is a living and personal energy, not a machine, and makes a response of love to all our movements of love – even the most babyish. But our power of interceding for those quite unknown to us is very closely connected with our membership of the Church – it is her total prayer in which we take part. As individualists we could not do it with any sense of reality. I think we have to try to keep two sorts of Intercession going – this share in the Church's prayer and also our personal self-offering for persons or causes about which we care deeply – the corporate and individual sides of full religion.

To S. T., 12 August 1940, *Letters*, pp. 292–3

# What Can Be Offered

Physical and mental labour, no less than spiritual labour, can become the vehicles of spiritual effectiveness: for the worth of intercession abides, not in the specific things which it can and does do for us, but in the unimpeded channel offered by its loving intention to the transforming Divine love and will. There is included in its work that strange power of one spirit to penetrate, illuminate, support and rescue other spirits, through which so much of the spiritual work of the world seems to be done; the more awful privilege of redemptive suffering, as it appears again and again in the lives of the saints; the total dedication of the contemplative, redressing in adoration the downward trend of our largely self-interested world; the strong out-streaming prayer of the cloistered nun, given for the general need. Not only these, but the scientist's costly battle with disease; the heroic reformer's struggle for social purity; the joyful endurance of physical pain and weakness which makes many a sick-bed into a radiant centre of spiritual power. By each such act and life the tiny human creature, if only for a moment, contributes to that spiritualizing of the natural order which 'takes away the sin of the world'.

'I believe', says Elisabeth Leseur, 'that there circulates among all souls, those here below, those who are being purified, and those who have achieved the true Life, a vast and ceaseless stream made of the sufferings, the merits, and the love of all those souls: and that even our smallest pains, our least efforts can, through the divine action, reach other souls both near and distant, and bring to them light, peace and holiness.'

All this must inevitably take place at a certain cost to the creature. Much that goes to make full natural life may be sacrificed; ease and liberty, family happiness, health. Creative and redemptive prayer has never been regarded by those called to it as a succession of interior delights. By their universal testimony it is often full of pain, bitterness and tension; though always proceeding from a spirit which is utterly at peace. For it carries a heavy burden, but carries it with joy.

*Man and the Supernatural*, pp. 259–60

# A Link With God's Grace

God's creative and transforming action does not seem to work as something separate from the souls of men and women, but in and through those souls of men and women. 'We are not,' said Baron von Hügel, 'to think of Spirit and spirit, God and the soul, as two separate entities. His Spirit works in closest association with ours.'

A real man or woman of prayer, then, should be a live wire, a link between God's grace and the world that needs it. In so far as you have given your lives to God, you have offered yourselves, without conditions, as transmitters of His saving and enabling love: and the will and love, the emotional drive, which you thus consecrate to God's purposes, can do actual work on supernatural levels for those for whom you are called upon to pray. One human spirit can, by its prayer and love, touch and change another human spirit; it can take a soul and lift it into the atmosphere of God. This happens, and the fact that it happens is one of the most wonderful things in the Christian life. All your prayers, and far more than that, all your generous and loving desires, trials, sufferings, fatigues and renunciations – and of course there is no real life of prayer without all these – can avail for those persons and causes you seek to help. To all of them you are, or should be, agents or transmitters of the transforming, redeeming power of God; and the most real work you ever do should be that which you do secretly and alone.

*Life as Prayer*, pp. 2–3

# Intercession and Spiritual Communion

The Christian fellowship, of which we are always hearing so much, is quite misunderstood, isn't it, if we think of it merely in terms of outward religious contact? For the real and vital communion between souls is invisible and spiritual – so deeply buried that we can think of it as existing unbroken below the changeful surface of daily life. External contact is at best only the outward sign of a far more profound inward grace – that mysterious interpenetration of all living souls, which is the secret of the Communion of Saints. And the whole possibility of intercessory prayer seems based on this truth of spiritual communion – the fact that we are *not* separate little units, but deeply interconnected – so that all we do, feel and endure has a secret effect, radiating far beyond ourselves. This is a thought that should help us when outward contacts are difficult or discouraging, or when circumstances limit our apparent 'scope.'

With some people this sympathetic contact with others actually reaches the conscious level. By their energy of love and pity they can enter and share the secret joys, needs, griefs, and temptations of those with whom they are placed, can knowingly stand by and give them support, and literally bear the weight and suffering of their griefs, sins, and disease. We have all seen a little of this strange faculty in devoted mothers, devoted friends, and sometimes, too, in ministers of religion. In the saints it develops a marvellous vividness and power. That conscious stretching out of the soul may mean much suffering for those who can do it; but it also means a wonderful sense of close communion both with humanity and with God. Such people know for certain that when we pray we are never alone, but enter a vast spiritual society where genuine work is done. By their prayers they can deeply influence those with whom they are in contact. They can fight battles for them in secret, rescue, heal them and give them to God.

*Life as Prayer*, pp. 3–5

# Redemptive Work

The human soul is one of the instruments through which the 'tranquil operations of His perpetual Providence' are performed. It is a living tool of the Holy Spirit which works in the world of prayer. All that it gains in its own secret life of adoration and communion it can and should give again to others in supernatural ways, thus becoming a real distributing centre of God's creative power. Drop by drop the enabling power of grace comes to us, and keeps on coming, out of the treasuries of the Eternal World — comes to us in our prayers and communions and in every opportunity of patience and sacrifice — and we can rely absolutely on that unfailing supply, provided that we spend it all again generously in redemptive work for the world, and especially for those to whom we are linked in prayer.

What we call 'influence' is just the faint outward expression, the crude hint, of one of the ways in which the soul can thus work in prayer. Influence is due to the fact that every living personality stretches out tentacles, as it were, to touch and penetrate surrounding personalities; and suggests the immense power which we can thus exercise. Even influence, then, is enough to prove that human souls are truly open to and affected by the moulding action of each other's love and prayer — that they can take colour, and draw energy and peace, from the personalities among whom they are placed. So, no break with our regular experience is involved in the belief that the spiritual development of men and women is largely effected by God through those among whom He has placed them.

Each time you take a human soul with you into your prayer, you accept from God a piece of spiritual work with all its implications and with all its cost — a cost which may mean for you spiritual exhaustion and darkness and may even include vicarious suffering, the Cross. In offering yourselves on such levels of prayer for the sake of others, you are offering to take your part in the mysterious activities of the spiritual world; to share the saving work of Christ. Each soul thus given to your care brings a need which it is your job to meet, and an opportunity which will never be repeated, a duty that no one else can fulfil.

*Life as Prayer*, pp. 5–7

# Costly Self-Surrender

Of course it is in the saints that we see this love, and this intercessory power, acting on highest levels and effecting marvellous transformations. To learn what they did and do in their prayers is to realize what great untapped sources of power are all about us, ready for us to use if we will pay the price – lose our separate lives that we may find life. Consider such cases as those of St Catherine of Siena, the young girl of the people whose spiritual transcendency transformed the ecclesiastical politics of her day, and who rescued countless sinners by her love and prayer: or the Curé d'Ars, the humble peasant priest who drew troubled souls from every corner of France and took on himself the burden of their sins; or Elizabeth Fry, going in the power of the Spirit to transform the awful life of the prisoners in Newgate Gaol. These, and countless others, make us realize how dreadfully shallow and careful, how ungenerous and untrusting our own little spiritual operations mostly are. Most of us do not really give our lives. At best we give a working day.

I am sure it was because the saints were so utterly uncalculating in their self-giving, cared for souls in such a divine way, and with such unmeasured love and eager acceptance of suffering, minded about people so much, that they did their great redeeming works of prayer. They show us that real intercession is not merely a petition but a piece of work, involving perfect, costly self-surrender to God for the work He wants done on other souls. Such great self-giving and great results may be their special privilege; still, they are showing us on a grand scale something which each cell of the Body of Christ has got to try to do on a small scale. They prove to us how closely and really all human spirits are connected – what we can do for one another if we only love enough – and how far-reaching is the power and responsibility of every Christian soul. We can only understand their experience by realizing that we are truly parts of a great spiritual organism. The Mystical Body of Christ is not an image, but a fact. We perpetually give and take from each other the indwelling Divine Life, and by our prayers, thoughts and actions affect all within our radius.

*Life as Prayer*, pp. 7–9

# Self-Offering and Sacrifice

Whenever love and religion transcend the self-regarding stage and anchor themselves on God, this sense that the soul is able to work and suffer for its fellows, and in some way share the eternal mystery of the Cross, seems to appear. I think none of us could deny that a strong redemptive and sacrificial element runs right through the best and deepest Christianity. The Christian religion is not just a beautiful system of ethics or a particular kind of belief about God. It is not only a devotion, however pure and loving, to the person of Christ. It does something to human nature which cannot be done in any other way. That sacrificial instinct so deeply planted in mankind, which finds such varied and strange expression as it follows the upward path of evolution – this it is which triumphs in the real intercessory life. Self-offering, loving, unconditional and courageous, is therefore the first requirement of true intercessory prayer. The interceding soul must be willing to go with our Lord to Gethsemane and Cavalry, and share with Him the crushing weight of the world's sin, disorder, disease.

That is a tremendous model to set before ourselves, isn't it? But, at any rate, it is a model that helps us most when we need it most. Just because it appeals to what is most heroic in us, it makes us glad and anxious to do such bits of this mysterious divine work as may fall to our share, whatever strain and renunciation they may require. We are here the assistants of that Good Shepherd who gives His life for the sheep.

*Life as Prayer*, pp. 10–11

# A Path to the Spirit

Now, if we are to offer ourselves for and in those sick and helpless sheep, we shall not do it only by deliberately religious deeds and thoughts; for no one, without unhealthy strain, can keep all his deeds and thoughts on the religious level all the time. We shall do it as human beings as well as spiritual beings. That is, by more and more giving spiritual and intercessory value to *all* the acts and intentions of life, however homely, practical and simple; lifting that whole life, visible and invisible, on to the sacramental plane, turning it into prayer.

Physical, mental and spiritual labour, with all the successes and failures, the difficulties, sufferings, demands on patience and humility that go with each kind, can all become the vehicles of our spiritual effectiveness; if every bit is given, by intention, for the good of those who are in our prayer. These things, which can all be the means of raising us towards God, must be the means of raising other souls at the same time. For the real worth of intercessions does not consist in the specific things we ask for or obtain, but in the channel offered by our love and sacrifice to the creative and redeeming love and will of God. We open a fresh path to His Spirit; make straight the way along which He reaches a needy soul, a struggling movement, or a desolate corner of life.

Perhaps the contact will be made through some act of loving service on our part. Perhaps it will be our disciplined spirit of joy and peace which reaches out to those who most deeply need that inner tranquility. Perhaps the contact will not be made outwardly at all, but secretly in the world of prayer. However it may be made, it is essential to realize that here it is our privilege to minister the supernatural – God, in His richness and wonder; that He is coming through us to other souls in the way in which they can bear it best. The steadfast pressure of the Divine Energy and Love, felt at different levels and in different ways right through creation, is finding in us a special path of discharge.

*Life as Prayer*, pp. 11–13

# Communion With Christ

Surely we need not be surprised if all this costs us a good deal; for real spiritual work taxes to the utmost the limited powers of the natural creature. It is using them on a fresh level, subjecting them to fresh strains. And this means that our preparation for it, if we are beginners, our maintenance in a fit condition for it if we are mature, is an important part of our religious life. It will not be managed merely by suitable reading, church attendance, prayer circles or anything of that kind; but only by faithful personal attention to God, constant and adoring recourse to Him, confident humble communion with Him. And the upkeep of this life-giving contact with the Eternal World, this secret intercourse with the living Christ, is a primary duty which we owe to those for whom we pray. The loving, enraptured vision of God, the limitless self-forgetful confidence in God, the generous desire to give without stint for His purposes – these are the sources of those intercessions which have power.

What quality, then, is it in us that can thus become the agent of the Divine creativity? Not our intellects, however brilliant; not our faith, however clear and correct; not our active works, however zealous. We may lack all these; and yet through us God's work may be done.

There is ultimately only one thing in us that can and will be used by God to carry His love and power from soul to soul, and that is the mysterious thing we call a consecrated personality. This is surely the lesson of the Incarnation – a lesson repeated again and again in the history of the Church. Not what Christ did and said, but what He was and is, guarantees God to us, and brings God's power to us. And similarly, on our own tiny scale, not what we say or do, but what we are, provides the medium through which God reaches those to whom we are sent. Thus we come back again, don't we? to the point at which we began; that the first duty of the intercessor is communion with that Spirit in Whom our being is. We must keep ourselves sensitive to the Eternal, delicately responsive to God.

*Life as Prayer*, pp. 13–15

# Eucharist: The Praying Church

There is no human situation or human need which lies outside the radius of the Divine Compassion, and cannot be the material of our intercessory care.

So the Christian communicant must become ever more sensitive to the pressure of this creative love, driving us to all possible objects of love, small as well as great. Those whose lives are self-offered on the altar of holy desire, are transferred once for all from the sphere of private enterprise to that of co-operative action. Natural and spiritual faculties and insights, the power of prayer, ghostly strength and skill, are now dedicated to the general purposes of the Eternal order, not to the special purposes and profit of the individual soul; who here dies to live, and must often be content with a spiritual poverty in order that others may be enriched. The seventeenth-century divines were fond of talking of the 'profits of Godliness.' But there are no personal profits in the Eucharistic life. They all go back into the business; and none would have it otherwise who have achieved even the beginnings of the spiritual self-oblivion which is the only source of spiritual peace. Here, all that is produced, done, offered or endured is added to the total oblation of the Praying Church, the total action of the Body of Christ. Only as a cell of that Body, a capacity for the Spirit, an agent of the supernatural action, can the individual soul intercede. It comes to offer the sacrifice, yet is itself part of the sacrifice. The Eucharistic life is not a devotional addition to existence, but the clue to all real existence whether social or personal. It is concerned with the mighty realities of evil and redemption, death and life. The more deeply the soul enters into the great movement of the Liturgy, the more this truth is experienced; and all devotional pettiness, all spiritual self-seeking purged away.

*The Mystery of Sacrifice*, pp. 35–6

# Eucharist: The Great Intercession

The Great Intercession is a prayer of creative desire; desire that the whole world may be brought to the altar of God and made ardent by the flame of His Charity, transforming all our activities and institutions and making them a part of the Kingdom of Heaven. In its movement towards God the soul made a first step towards the transcendence of egotism; here, it makes the second step. The second commandment comes immediately after the first. We are to turn from our own spiritual interests, our own devotional attractions, and bring all life into our prayer, that we may lift it towards God: thus enlarging that charity which is the substance of our spiritual life in two directions, not only in one. This wide and generous spirit of love, not the religious egotist's longing to get away from the world to God, is the fruit of true self-oblation; for a soul totally possessed by God is a soul totally possessed by Charity. By the path of self-offering the Church and the soul have come up to the frontiers of the Holy. There, we are required, not to cast the world from us, but do our best for others as well as ourselves; as Christ was self-offered for others and prayed for others in the hour of His sacrifice, and sanctified Himself for their sakes. 'The altar,' said St Catherine of Siena, 'is the Table of Holy Desire – desire for the honour of God and for the health and salvation of souls.' The two go together. Real adoration never forgets its familial obligation to the other children of the Beloved. Our desire is to be offered on this table, that it may be cleansed, transformed, unselfed, united with the Divine creative desire, and devoted to the purposes of God. All this is a true part of the reasonable sacrifice; a necessary function of the Eucharistic life.

*The Mystery of Sacrifice*, pp. 31–2

# Eucharist: Redeeming Power

Each soul which is subdued to the Eucharistic rhythm must complete the first small movement of generosity towards God by the compensating movement of generosity to all men and women. Being given to Him, she is at once put to work. Her self-offering has made her a tool and channel of the Divine Charity; of mercy, healing, and redeeming power. She is now required to remember, not merely her own spiritual hunger and weakness, but her fellow creatures and their most homely needs; for, since all spirits are united within the Charity of God, and all are created that they may be the agents of His Love, the sacrificial act, the loving inclination of even one humble soul does something for all. The Eucharistic life is profoundly social; the wide compass and the backward and forward sweep of those intercessory prayers which appear, in one form or another, in all liturgies, assure us of that.

So the Great Intercession, placed at the very heart of the Eucharist, to check as it were the forward rush of the soul towards God, reminds us that Christianity is not a religion of escape; that it accepts the full burden, fret and responsibility of humanity, does not evade it. The Christian communicant goes to the altar as a member of the family; not as one who has contracted out of the family life. He goes to offer himself to that God, who in Christ reconciled the world to Himself. Intercession, therefore, embraces the whole world in its scope; not only the hopeful causes, but the hopeless, not only the respectable but the disgraceful. The confusions, sins, and cruelties; the people and policies that we should prefer to forget; the horrors, the failures, the short ends. All these it can, by the mysterious power of sacrifice, lift up and reconcile to God.

*The Mystery of Sacrifice*, pp. 32–4

# Eucharist: Praying from the Cross

'Hitherto,' says Christ to His disciples, entrusting them with the continuance of His redemptive prayer, 'you have asked nothing in My Name.' You are now to ask in the Name of the Crucified, to pray from the Cross. The cost is great. The response is certain, though it may be a response that we do not recognize. For Christian intercession is the completion and expression of self-giving. It means that the soul offers its imperfect love as a channel and vehicle of God's perfect love. It is the stretching out of the arms upon the cross of life, that they may embrace the whole world. It means the soul's desire and effort given generously and unconditionally, not in view of its own spiritual achievement, its own movement towards communion with God, but wholly for His mysterious purposes; redemptive, sacrificial prayer as an essential factor in all self-oblation – the human creature self-emptied, and made a channel of the Divine action through which God reaches out to the sins and needs of the world.

The soul, then, which is called to intercessory action must be willing not only to pray from the Cross, in unquestioning self-abandonment, but also to share the agony, darkness, loneliness and disillusionment of the Cross; for only thus can its saving power be actualized. Evil itself, and the taint, horror and penalty of evil, it may be required to draw into the purifying flame of love; the assault of temptation, the revolt, the dread and helplessness, the pain and intimate pressure of sin, that all this may be burnt upon the altar of sacrifice. We are far from realizing yet what human beings can do for one another in the world of sacrificial prayer; but the Liturgy never allows us to forget the central place which it holds in the Eucharistic response of Church and soul to God.

Fastidious prayer, concentration on purely spiritual needs, aloofness from the homely interests of the temporal world, are therefore hostile to the spirit of the Liturgy. The whole rich tangle of creation, loved and supported by God, must be the concern of all who are given to God.

*The Mystery of Sacrifice*, pp. 33–5

# Intercession: Praying from the Cross

Personal worship is exercised in two directions: vertically in adoration, and horizontally in intercession . . . True intercessors offer the oblation of their imperfect love, that it may become a channel of the Absolute Love. Here they pray from the Cross. According to the degree of their self-offering is the power of their prayer; and a part of their self-offering will be an entire willingness to work and suffer in the dark, asking for no assurance of result. All that they do and endure, is done and endured as the adoring tools and servants of Creative Love; and in the last result, their intercessory action is part of the movement of Its Will . . . It is those who best practise the loving adoration who will best practise the loving expansion; since dwelling in Charity they dwell in God, and become effective channels of His generosity. At their full development the two movements are merged in that one, all-inclusive act of self-giving and obedient love, which Christians find revealed in the life of Jesus and supremely expressed in the Cross: the arms stretched out to embrace the world, and the eyes lifted up towards the Eternal God.

*Worship*, pp. 167–8

# WAR — AND PEACE

Sir Arthur Underhill, *writing in his autobiography of the different ways in which the air raids during World War I affected people's nerves, paints a picture of his family's reactions which may surprise us: 'My wife was calm but terrified, and loathed the raids, but my daughter, I think, really enjoyed them.'*[1]

*It is difficult to conceive of the Evelyn Underhill we know as enjoying anything to do with war; and as other evidence seems to indicate that neither of her parents ever really understood or empathized with her, her true feelings were probably misconstrued.*

*Certainly in those days she had not embraced her later pacifist stance. During World War I she was intensely patriotic, even working for Naval Intelligence. In her writing, her emphasis was not on the denunciation of war per se, but of 'fair weather Christians' who could not reconcile the practice of prayer with the perpetration of such atrocities. It was part of true patriotism, Evelyn said, 'to keep the spiritual life, both of the individual and of the social group, active and vigorous.'*[2]

*In the Preface to* Practical Mysticism *(published in 1914), as in her paper the following year,* Mysticism and War, *she stressed that, 'The spiritual life is not a special career, involving abstraction from the world of things'.*[3] *She was effectually defending mysticism against the 'charge' of pacifism, and clearly indicating where she stood on the subject at that stage of her life. The mystics she described were tremendous patriots, 'happy warriors,' who combined the active and contemplative lives even in wartime. Indeed, war seemed to give them the chance to let their lights really shine!*

*In the 1930s, her attitude changed completely. Her last spiritual director, Reginald Somerset Ward, was a true pacifist, and Aldous Huxley's pamphlet,* What Are You Going To Do About It? *(1936) probably completed her 'conversion'. She became a member of the Peace Pledge Union and, in 1939, of the Anglican Pacifist Fellowship. She proceeded to write much on this subject:* A Meditation on Peace *(1939),* Prayer in Wartime *(1939),* Spiritual Life in Wartime *(1939), and* The Church and War *(1940). Her stand was unmistakable and uncompromising: war is* sin; *war is* evil.

*It had the capacity to bring out the best in people — she was*

[ 148 ]

thrilled, for example, by the stories of selfless heroism at Dunkirk – but mainly war highlighted the lack of faith both of individuals and of the Church.

> [London] really does feel like living in the Inferno, perpetually confronted by the folly and wickedness of humankind . . . Christians never (or hardly ever) seem able to take the gift of Power seriously . . . It is because our Christianity is so impoverished, so second-hand and non-organic, that we now feel we are incapable of the transformation of life which is needed to get humanity out of its present mess. It all comes back of course to the lack of a concrete, realistic faith.[4]

Evelyn suffered dreadfully through the war. Her external physical privations were probably neither more nor less than anyone else's; and though she accepted them heroically, she felt them keenly. Even the prohibitive cost of stamps served as an isolating element, depriving her of much congenial communication with the friends from whom she was separated.

Her letters give us an idea of her stoicism and faith:

> The whole district is practically without water since the Highgate Power Station was blown up last week. We fill buckets from the main in the morning and live on it as best we can during the day. However there is a certain odd satisfaction in being reduced to primitive conditions and having to practice abstinence about something one has always taken for granted. Sitting very loose to possessions and much simplification of life is certainly one of the lessons the Lord is going to teach us through the war, and we are beginning to get on with it now.[5]

Most difficult to accept was the 'betrayal' of her once-pacifist friends:

> So many of my fellow pacifists seem to have fallen from the absolute position and think that Hitler's wickedness justifies participation in the war; but when we have won it they will be pacifists again. I cannot feel, however, that committing sin to cure sin is either Christianity or common sense, and the steady increase in bombast and self-righteous heroics is very displeasing, isn't it? Perhaps we have reached a level of collective sinfulness in which we cannot do right.[6]

Health and friends may have failed her, but Evelyn's integrity, courage and love for God and others did not. A month before her death, she wrote:

> I feel more and more sure that Christianity and war are incompatible, and that nothing worth having can be achieved by 'casting out Satan by Satan.' All the same . . . at present I think one can do little but try to live in charity, and do what one can for the suffering and bewildered . . . Let us hope that the end of all the horror and destruction may be a purification of life.[7]

Her mission in her last days was as it had been all her life: 'To adhere to the Eternal God, and help others to steady their lives in the same way.'[8]

1. Sir Arthur Underhill, *Change and Decay*, p. 110.
2. Evelyn Underhill, *Practical Mysticism*, p. x.
3. *ibid.* p. ix.
4. Charles Williams (ed), *The Letters of Evelyn Underhill*, pp. 296–7
5. *ibid.* p. 295.
6. *ibid.* pp. 299–300.
7. *ibid.* p. 308.
8. *ibid.* p. 305.

# The Christian Perspective on War

War is sin worked out to its inevitable conclusion in violence, hatred, greed and mutual mistrust: part of a deeper disharmony, a split between the whole created order and the Divine Charity, an orientation of life towards self-satisfaction, national or personal, and away from God. Thus even the most just of wars implies a movement away from Christ, from His spirit, method and aims; but peace is one point in the Church's great effort to 'restore all things in him'. Wars and fighting, says St James, are always suspect in origin . . .

War then is the material expression of spiritual sin, the deflection of the great powers of initiative, the great control of physical resources, which have been entrusted to us from serving God's purpose to accomplishing our own. Its causes are rooted in possess- iveness, in inordinate desire – the frenzied clutch on what we have, the desperate grab at what we have not. But Christianity, considered as a clue to life's meaning, has no more interest in the clutch than in the grab. From first to last it urges detachment from possessions, and will only impart its deepest secrets to those who are willing to leave all. It does not merely regulate possessiveness, but it transcends it. Its response to greed is generosity. 'If any would take away thy coat let him have thy cloak also' (Matthew 5:40). Don't stand on your rights, or defend your own – all is God's.

'Postscript' from *Into the Way of Peace* by
Percy Hartill (ed.), pp. 189–90

# The Real Mission: Wisdom and Love

[Christians] are bound to repudiate war, not only in principle but also in fact. The reason, for there is only one, is simple and conclusive. The Christian Church is the Body of Christ. Her mission on earth is to spread the Spirit of Christ, which is the creative spirit of wisdom and love; and in so doing, bring in the Kingdom of God. Therefore she can never support or approve any human action, individual or collective, which is hostile to wisdom and love.

This is the first and last reason why, if she remains true to her supernatural call, the Church cannot acquiesce in war. For war, however camouflaged or excused, must always mean the effort of one group of people to achieve their purpose – get something which they want, or prevent something happening which they do not want – by inflicting destruction and death on another group.

*The Church and War*, p. 1

# The Folly of the Cross

Christianity alone holds the solutions of humanity's most terrible and most pressing problem. She alone has something practical to say, for to her has been confided the Word of God. It is the Church's hour; and she will not face it, because like the hour of birth it means risk, travail, inevitable pain. We are forced to the bitter conclusion that the members of the Visible Church as a body are not good enough, nor brave enough to risk everything for that which they know to be the Will of God and the teaching of Christ. For it does mean risking everything: freedom, reputation, friendship, security – life itself. It is the folly of the Cross, in the particular form in which our generation is asked to accept it; that absolute choice which the Rich Young Man could not make. 'If I were still pleasing men, I should not be the slave of Christ,' said St Paul to the Galatians. The Church is still very busy pleasing men.

*The Church and War,* p. 4

# No War is Righteous

When we trace war to its origin, that origin is always either mortal sin – Pride, Anger, Envy, Greed – or else that spirit of self-regarding Fear, which is a worse infidelity to God than any mortal sin. The Christian cannot serve these masters, even though they are wearing national dress. The Christian attitude to the use of violence, 'justifiable' or 'unjustifiable', was settled once and for all in Gethsemane. Our Lord's rebuke to St Peter condemns all 'righteous' wars, or resort to arms, even in the defence of the just and the holy. No cause could indeed have been more just and holy than that of the disciples who sought to defend the Redeemer from His enemies; from their point of view, they would have been fighting for the Kingdom of God, and the highest claims of patriotism must fade before this. Yet it was not by any resort to arms that the world was to be saved; but by the suffering, patience, and sacrificial love of the Cross.

*The Church and War*, p. 1

# God Loves All Creation

Christians are bound to the belief that all creation is dear to the Creator, and is the object of His cherishing care. The violent as well as the peaceful, the dictators as well as their victims, the Blimps as well as the pacifists, the Government as well as the Opposition, the sinners as well as the saints. All are children of the Eternal Perfect. Some inhabitants of this crowded nursery are naughty, some stupid, some wayward, some are beginning to get good. God loves, not merely tolerates, these wayward, violent, half-grown spirits; and seeks without ceasing to draw them into His love. We, then, are called to renounce hostile attitudes and hostile thoughts towards even our most disconcerting fellow sinners; to feel as great a pity for those who go wrong as for their victims, to show an equal generosity to the just and unjust. This is the only peace-propaganda which has creative quality, and is therefore sure of ultimate success. All else is scratching on the surface, move likely to irritate than to heal.

*A Meditation on Peace*, pp. 2–3

# No Retaliation

To defeat the power of evil by the health-giving power of love and thus open a channel for the inflow of the creative grace of God is therefore the only struggle in which the realistic Christian can take part. No retaliation. No revenge, national or personal. No 'defensive wars' – i.e. destroying our brother to prevent him from destroying us. 'Fear not him that can kill the body' says the Church – or so at least the Church ought to say. Yet armament factories working fulltime announce to the world that we do fear him very much indeed; and are determined, if it comes to the point, to kill his body before he can kill ours. The attitude is one with which the Christian Church must never come to terms; the questions of expediency, practicality, national prestige and national safety do not as such concern her. All these derive from human egotism and human fear. Her single business is to apply everywhere and at all times the law of charity; and so bring the will of man, whether national or individual, into harmony with the Will of God . . . [The Church] will not make her message effective, until she shows the courage of her convictions and makes her own life, individual and corporate, entirely consistent with the mandate she has received. She cannot minister with one hand the Chalice of Salvation, whilst with the other she blesses the instruments of death.

*The Church and War*, p. 2

# No Compromise

The Church is in the world to save the world. The whole of human life is her province, because Christianity is not a religion of escape but a religion of incarnation; not standing alongside human life, but working in and through it. So, she is bound to make a choice and declare herself on the great issues of that life, and carry through her choice into action, however great the cost. War means people pressing their own claims and demands, or resisting others' claims and demands, to the point of destruction. At best this is atavism, at worst it is devilry. The individual sacrifices for which it calls are sacrifices indeed; but they are not made at the only altar which Christians can acknowledge – the altar of Divine Love. Therefore the Church cannot acquiesce in war; nor can any communicant who is true to the costly realities of faith take part in it. Christianity stands for absolute values, and the Church falls from grace every time she compromises about them; for she is a supernatural society, consisting of persons who have crossed over from the world's side and have accepted service under the august standard of the Cross, with all that service of the Cross implies. Necessarily though in the world, the Church can never be of it. For the world detests absolute values; they are so inconvenient. 'Marvel not, my brethren, if the world hates you.'

*The Church and War*, pp. 2–3

# Creative Peace

Peace and Joy are permanent characters of a realistic Christianity; the inseparable signs of the Spirit's presence in the soul. They are not achieved at the end of our growth; but are present from the beginning, hidden in the deeps, long before the restless surface mind is able to receive them. One of the German confessional pastors imprisoned for his faith wrote home saying, 'though on the surface it may be rough weather, twenty fathoms down it is quite calm.' That's it. There, beyond succession, where the soul's ground touches essential Being, it is the inexhaustible fount of peace. There it must be nourished, by contemplation, not be negotiation; and thence it must radiate in slowly spreading circles, at last to conquer the unpeaceful world.

Such creative peace, if it is indeed brought forth by the Spirit, will mean an entire and tranquil acquiescence in the action or nonaction of God; not merely as regards our own lives but, what is far more difficult, as regards the sufferings, sins and conflicts of the world. A peace and joy which endures in and through the compassion, indignation, helplessness and puzzle of mind with which we see the cruelty and injustice of life, the violence of the strong, the anguish of the weak and the oppressed. Even this pain and evil, and the world's dark future, we are to realise as enfolded in a deeper, imperishable life; and it is when we see it thus, from God's side, that we deal with its problems best.

*A Meditation on Peace*, p. 3

# True Pacifism

One thing about [pacifism] which matters supremely [is] its relation to the total Christian revelation of God's nature as absolute love. For pacifism is only on safe ground where it is based on and embodies these eternal principles; and is seen, not in isolation as an attitude towards the particular problem of war, but as part of the great task committed to humanity – the bringing forth of eternal life in the midst of time, or the setting up of the Kingdom of God. The doctrine of nonresistance is after all merely a special application of the great doctrine of universal charity; and it is of the utmost importance that pacifists should escape from their own little paddock and realise this. The fact that so many pacifists felt obliged to abandon the absolute position when the present war increased in intensity and disclosed to us the full possibilities and results of military defeat, shows how few had really based their convictions on these eternal principles, how much expediency was still mingled with their faith. Many were found willing when it came to the point to cast out Satan by Satan, rather than accept the awful risk inherent in the unlimited application of life to the doctrine of Christian love – that rational or personal crucifixion which may be the reward of absolute trust in the power of the Divine Charity, and absolute surrender to its claims.

Since all Christians are now agreed on the wrongfulness and wastefulness of war, even though they may in particular instances believe themselves compelled to wage it, acquiescence in this supposed necessity can only mean capitulation to expediency and defective confidence in God. True pacifism is one expression among many of this complete confidence, of that belief in the power and priority of the supernatural order which is the backbone of religion; and without such belief, it cannot long endure. It is a courageous affirmation of Love, Joy and Peace as ultimate characters in the real world of spirit; a refusal to capitulate to the world's sin and acquiesce in the standards of a fallen race.

'Postscript' from *Into the Way of Peace* by
Percy Hartill (ed.), pp. 187–8

# The True Pacifist

The pacifist is one who has crossed over to God's side and stands by the Cross, which is at once the supreme expression of that charity and the pattern of an unblemished trust in the Unseen. Thence, with eyes cleansed by prayer, he sees all life in supernatural regard; and knows that, though our present social order may crash in the furies of a total war and the darkness of Calvary may close down on the historic scene, the one thing that matters is the faithfulness of the creature to its own fragmentary apprehensions of the law of charity and its ultimate return to the tranquillity of order, which is a perfect correspondence with the steadfast Will of God. His or her pacifism, then, is a judgment on existence. It is rooted in God and can only maintain itself by that contemplation which St Gregory calls the 'vision of the principle'. It is not a practical, this-world expedient for getting the best results from our human situation; though indeed it is true that no other ordering of our existence can produce the best results.

So once more true pacifism discloses itself as a supernatural vocation, a bringing of ultimate truth into the world of time, demanding of those who embrace it unlimited faith, unshakable hope, inexhaustible charity. For it means complete and confident self-giving to the methods and purposes of God; a break with human prudence and the gospel of safety first. It is a positive and creative direction for living, poised on the unseen future; and involves much more than the mere repudiation of war.

'Postscript' from *Into the Way of Peace* by
Percy Hartill (ed.), pp. 188–9

# LETTERS OF DIRECTION

*Letter-writing was a tremendously important part of Evelyn's life, and it was an essential function of her role as a spiritual director. From the numerous letters of direction we find in Charles Williams' edited collection of her* Letters, *it is possible to make a study of her approach to spiritual direction, to gain a living picture of Evelyn as a person and as a director. We are also able to deduce some of the problems that beset her in her own spiritual journey.*

*Evelyn regarded letter-writing as a sacred duty; and she understood what a vital lifeline of communication and comfort to others were 'those letters which are the mysterious link between soul and soul'.*[1]

*Much of Evelyn's correspondence, as we might expect, was with close friends – some of whom also looked to her for spiritual advice. Others – some of whom eventually* became *friends – began as enquirers. We see the beginnings of many such relationships in the* Letters, *a notable one being 'M.R.' (Margaret Robinson), who wrote to Evelyn in 1904 to congratulate her on the publication of her first novel,* The Grey World, *and at the same time disclosed her own state of 'spiritual unrest' and her need of help. Eventually she became Evelyn's 'secretary' and assistant in the research for* Mysticism, *a friend as well as a directee. We are indebted to M.R. for having preserved thirty-eight of Evelyn's letters, all but one written between 1904 and 1912, which comprise the bulk of the first section of the* Letters, *and demonstrate her competence as a director, even in the early days. In M.R.'s case, as in many others, the letters bridged the gap between personal interviews, which were usually conducted at Evelyn's Campden Hill Square home. Where there was a genuine need, Evelyn responded to the urgency of the situation – sometimes we find letters of direction written to the same person, with only a few days between them. It is an interesting and profitable exercise to go through the* Letters *(which are arranged chronologically except for a collection at the end written to Lucy Menzies), picking out all those written to a particular person, to examine the correspondence as a whole. It is then possible to gain a picture of the person to whom Evelyn is writing and, in some cases, to trace a problem through to its conclusion.*

We realize too that she was dealing with the same or similar problems in many different individuals.

In this chapter we have just a small selection from a few of the individuals she helped, like her 'poor lamb', 'D.E.', facing up to God's call to total sacrifice with fear and apprehension, and much in need of Evelyn's comforting 'paw in the dark'. (Evelyn loved cats, and frequently used imagery and analogies relating to her favourite animals.)

So many of Evelyn's directees, like 'W.Y.', were too self-occupied and self-analytical, obsessed with the idea of making 'progress,' and depressed when the results weren't what they wanted to see. Evelyn constantly and wisely advises avoiding strain, discourages the use of self-imposed penances (even 'verbal hair-shirts'!), recommends taking greater care of the body, and, even, having fun! With her typical combination of humour and practical common sense she orders 'W.Y.' to 'check the habit of getting the bulb out of the dark to see how it is getting on' – useful analogy for the fruitless endeavours we so often undertake when we try to do things our own way, only ending up anxious and frustrated. Even intellectual conviction cannot be forced, as we see in the advice given to 'A.M.J.'. Time and again Evelyn reminds her directees – and us – that God gives such light as is needed; our part is to trust, and to rest in him.

Nearly all Evelyn's directees were women; and one can understand how grateful they must have been to find someone in the male-dominated Church of the first three decades of this century, to whom they could relate. Evelyn combined a sense of humour with common sense, and tender compassion with clarity and discernment. This could mean that a letter which begins: 'My poor lamb, I am so terribly sorry for you . . .', is within two lines uncompromisingly reminding the 'poor lamb' that, 'If you choose Christ you start on a route that goes over Calvary'.[2]

Evelyn's own deep spirituality could point in only one direction: towards God. Her advice is timeless. If we read her letters with humility, discernment, and openness, we shall hear the voice of God in them as surely today as Evelyn's directees did then.

1. Evelyn Underhill, *The Mount of Purification*, p. 78.
2. Charles Williams (ed.), *The Letters of Evelyn Underhill*, p. 224.

# Seeking the Light

I must thank you very much for writing to me as kindly as you have done. I think it is so good of those who have read, and have cared for what they have read, to write and tell the author, who knows little of what her work is doing, once it has gone out into the world. As you say, the finding of reality is the one thing that matters, and that always mattered, though it has been called by many different names.

Of course, on this side of the veil, the perfect accomplishment of the quest is impossible; we can only come to the edge of the sea that separates us from the City of Sarras. Few get so far, but for those who do, it seems that there is a certain hope. It is of course quite difficult for me, from one letter, to judge of your position; so I hope you will forgive me if I say anything you do not like.

But you say in one place, that the more urgent the want of reality grows, the less you see how to effect it. Now, this state of 'spiritual unrest' can never bring you to a state of vision, of which the essential is peace. And struggling to see does not help one to see. The light comes, when it does come, rather suddenly and strangely I think. It is just like falling in love; a thing that never happens to those who are always trying to do it.

You say also, as regards beauty, that you find its sensuous side dangerous and distracting. This is true at first; but when once it has happened to you to perceive that beauty is the 'outward and visible sign' of the greatest of sacraments, I don't think you can ever again get hopelessly entangled by its merely visible side. The real difficulty seems to me to come from the squalor and ugliness with which people try to overlay the world in which they live.

I have been so much interested by your letter and hope you will forgive this imperfect reply.

Perhaps you will write to me again when you are in the mood. Those who are on the same road can sometimes help one another.

To M.R., 29 November 1904, *Letters*, p. 51

# Self-Oblation and Un-Selfing

I'm so glad you wrote, and hope you always will when you feel the need of a paw in the dark. Anyhow this time the paw gives you a very pleased squeeze, and says, 'All's well!' Every word you say in your letter goes to prove that. It is a tough noviciate but a real one; and all the dark and humiliation (but what a lot of light and love there is with it too) is the shadow and tension which must come with God's direct dealing with the soul. He is showing you things very quickly now and opening new paths and opportunities of self-oblation. Don't be discouraged if you get a bit breathless or even fall flat on your face now and then. Far better, more alive, more demanding, and more utterly purifying from self-love than that 'blissful era of peace' you thought might come. You have so much to bring to the altar in the way of love, sympathy, compassion, all of which can be used by God through your intercessions. But while things are moving at this pace, please be careful not to overstrain. If your rule of life merely irks you – stick it out; but if it really strains (and perhaps it may) then modify it a bit. And above all, proper recreation, a day off if possible from taxing jobs, and ample sleep!

No – we can *never* become un-selfed on our own – it is God's work in us. We can only open the door and say, 'Do what You like.' Stick to your Chapman – he is a safe guide – and if you want another book, Grou's *Spiritual Maxims* will do well.

To D.E., 20 June 1933, *Letters*, p. 220

# Self-Occupation and Trust in God

I have liked your last two letters so much: the first I left unanswered according to your orders, but should like to say something about the one that came to-day.

1. Please at once check the habit of getting the bulb out of the dark to see how it is getting on! It is impossible, and also undesirable for you to judge your own progress. Just go along simply, humbly, naturally, and when tempted to self-occupation of this or any other sort, make a quiet act of trust in God. So long as you care to go along under my advice, it is my job and not yours to watch your soul and you may be quite sure I shall speak promptly when I am dissatisfied! Your faults and old fixations are going to give you lots of trouble for quite a long time and it's part of your job *not* to get discouraged. You will be much stronger and more useful to God in the end, for having had something to contend with.

2. But do please distinguish between faults and temperamental bias. There's nothing *wicked* in disliking current institutional religion (except Holy Communion). Your religion must of course have *some* institutional element; but it is particularly important that this element should not be overdone; and it certainly is not to be used as a penance. I think a sufficient institutional rule for *you* is to go to Church always once on Sunday, and this should be to Holy Communion by preference when obtainable. You have family worship at home; and let that, and perhaps some occasional service you may care to attend, suffice. The (quite natural) horror of seeming pious will wear off gradually as you settle down into the joy and peace of your new life.

I wonder whether you realize the extraordinary support and grace you have been given in your home atmosphere? The bulb has been put in the dark in a room with central heating so to speak, instead of the usual cold shed. I did so love all you said about your mother and wish I could know her. She must be the greatest of helps to you and of course can solve all your tangles if you talk to her freely. There's nothing more lovely is there than such a perfect Christian old age.

To W.Y., All Souls' Day, 1925, *Letters*, pp. 169–70

# Seeking Further Light

Thank you very much for your letter, and for writing as frankly as you have done. It is not easy to advise someone otherwise unknown on a sample letter, so if what I say does not meet the case, I hope you will write again. I have been during my life (I am now approaching sixty) through many phases of religious belief and I now realize – have done in fact for some time – that human beings can make little real progress on a basis of vague spirituality. God and the soul, and prayer as the soul's life, and the obligation of responding to God's demand, are real facts – in fact the most real of all facts – and they are the facts with which orthodox religion deals. As to dogmas which you cannot accept – e.g. the Virgin Birth – it is useless to force yourself on these points. Leave them alone for the time being, neither affirming nor rejecting them, and give your mind and will to living in harmony with those truths which you *do* see. This is the way – in fact the only way – to get further light.

For your own reading I think if you do not know them you would find Baron von Hügel's *Letters*, Dr Temple's *Christian Faith and Life*, the *Letters* of St Francis de Sales, and Grou's *Hidden Life of the Soul* valuable. You probably know the *Confessions* of St Augustine, but if not do study it. When you speak of reading more than you practise in your life, you put your finger on a real source of spiritual weakness. You would benefit by a simple rule of life: so much *definite* time each day given to prayer and spiritual reading; *definite* acts of, e.g. charity, self-denial, patience, aimed at 'mortifying' whatever your special faults of character may be. The 'active' and 'passive' sides of your nature are meant to collaborate, not compete! As to Holy Communion, consider that this is the way in which Christians have always drawn near to God, offered themselves to Him and received from Him spiritual food. Leave the more doctrinal side alone for the present, and go humbly, taking no notice of how you 'feel.' This really matters very little!

To A.M.J., 13 December 1934, *Letters*, pp. 239–40

# The Willingness to Suffer (1)

... You have made me understand your whole position ever so much more clearly by what you have told me; and I do thank you for your frankness and confidence. Very often one feels one is floundering in the dark when trying to help people, because there is some vital situation in the background which has not been disclosed. Now I know just where you are and also that you have (or have been *given* rather) the courage to do the right thing, in cutting this friendship out of your life. I know in such cases it seems a hard and even cruel thing to do or advise. But the fact remains that a competing emotional interest though technically 'innocent' can't be kept in one's life once one has given oneself to God. This very friendship may, later, return to you in the tranquil and purified form in which all one's human loves can be woven into the substance of the spiritual life. But as things are now, I am sure you are right in feeling that a clean cut is the only way. The fruit of all you experienced at Pleshey really hangs on your willingness to make the first definite sacrifice asked: and that you *have* made it, is the best of guarantees for your future steadiness. Moreover the pain you quite naturally dread won't be, in the event, so hard as it looks now. It is the *willingness* to suffer God asks. When we accept that, His grace comes with the pain and mysteriously takes away the real bitterness. Once the thing is done, you will know a new serenity, far better worth having than what you have given up: and all that is true and pure in this friendship will live on as a spiritual and unbreakable link and influence even through many years of silence and separation.

To A.B., 1 August 1927, *Letters*, pp. 174–5

# The Willingness to Suffer (2)

Now as to your future course:

1. I don't think you should, at present anyhow, try to 'go on alone.' You must expect ups and downs, difficulties, etc. – and it is much better you should have someone to whom you can tell them and who can look at your situation in a detached way. So I hope you will continue to write when you feel it is necessary.

2. Yes, I am sure your feeling that you should do some kind of spiritual work is sound and there is no reason to think that what you are most drawn to (Intercession and Healing) is unsuitable. On the contrary, other things being equal, one should always first try to follow one's spiritual *attrait*; though moderately and gradually, *not* exclusively and vehemently! So go gently in this direction, in the way and degree in which God suggests and opens ways for you, but balance it by your personal communion with Our Lord, in prayer, sacraments and reasonable voluntary renunciations.

3. (Of great importance.) Develop and expand the wholesome, natural and intellectual interests of your life – don't allow yourself to concentrate on the religious side only. Remember *all* life comes to you from God, and is to be used for Him – so live in it all, and so get the necessary variety and refreshment without which religious intensity soon becomes stale and hard . . . You will in this way retain, in the long run, far more of the sense of God's Presence than you would get from feverish concentration on it. Religious fervour eludes us when we chase it; but creeps back unawares. It is crucial that you should get these truths firmly fixed in your mind *now*, as they will have to govern your conduct (and so your growth) for years to come.

God bless you.

To A.B., 1 August 1927, *Letters*, p. 175

# Real Love

. . . Here is *The Cloud of Unknowing*: *Abandonment* is out at the moment, so that must wait till the autumn, but I am sending de Caussade's other one, on Prayer. You will find Part II the most interesting. I am also sending you, as a little present, my last book. If it does not agree with you, throw it away and don't force yourself to read it. But I think you may like the last part.

As to your question: yes, surely all generous, self-giving love, with no claimfulness, *is* part of God's love – 'who dwelleth in love dwelleth in God' -- any kind of real love! That is surely what St John is always trying to say. 'God is greater than our heart.'

As to all the rest, be content with this. God is enlightening you and teaching you direct, bit by bit as you can bear it. It *will* feel uncomfortable, you often *will* feel lost, ashamed and contrite. But all that is a great grace for which you must be very grateful, because it comes from the contrast between the great God deigning to touch you, and your small soul. It is for Him to choose what He shall show you, for you just to accept His lights and *gently* purify your love. It is natural and right that the soul should desire Him in Himself *and also* to be used by Him. Both these phases are part of a full spiritual life. But our longing for Him must be the kind that longs first for His will to be done, even though it means darkness for ourselves – at least that is how it seems to me.

Don't strain after more light than you've got yet: just wait quietly. God holds you when you cannot hold Him, and when the time comes to jump He will see to it that you *do* jump – and you will find you are not frightened then. But probably all that is a long way ahead still. So just be supple in His hands and let Him mould you (as He is doing) for His own purposes, responding with very simple acts of trust and love.

To L.K., 20 July 1923, *Letters*, pp. 212–13

# The Power of Prayer

I am sure the disciplined life based on the Sermon on the Mount is not easy! After all, it was never intended to be, was it? If you get an hour a day (as much as possible consecutive and in the morning) you ought I think to be able to handle the situation even though just now the 'sacrament of the present moment' may take rather a knobbly sort of form. Still God is in it – and it is there that you have to find a way of responding to Him and receiving Him and are actually being fed by Him. Christianity does mean getting down to actual ordinary life as the medium of the Incarnation, doesn't it, and our lessons in that get sterner, not more elegant as time goes on?

As to deliberate mortifications – I take it you do feel satisfied that you accept *fully* those God sends. That being so, you might perhaps do one or two little things, as acts of love, and also as discipline? I suggest by preference the mortification of the Tongue – as being very tiresome and quite harmless to the health. Careful guard on all amusing criticisms of others, on all complaints however casual and trivial; deliberately refraining sometimes (*not* always!) from saying the entertaining thing. This does not mean you are to be dull or correct, but to ration this side of your life! I doubt whether things like sitting on the least comfortable chair, etc., affect you enough to be worth bothering about! But I'm sure custody of the Tongue (on the lines suggested) could give you quite a bit of trouble and be a salutary bit of discipline, a sort of verbal hair-shirt. I think God does provide quite a reasonable amount of material for self-denial, etc, in your life. This extra bit is for love.

To. L.K., Lammas Day, 1937, *Letters*, p. 259

# The Sacrament of the Present Moment

. . . I think, about suffering, we can offer it to God for 'a particular intention' without any suggestion of bargaining – which would, of course, be horrible. We offer it as a kind of prayer – sometimes the only kind we *can* offer – 'I offer you this suffering which I accept and bear – I offer it as my prayer for so-and-so. Please take it and use it.' Specially we can offer it surely – because we are 'members of Christ,' as an atonement for sin – this, I suppose, is what St Catherine meant when she used to say to the naughty, '*I* will bear the burden of your sin.' Offering it for a definite object will, of course, like all intercession, be in subservience to the Will of God – which makes it all right.

As to that spiritual suffering you speak of, I think it is what some souls, not all, are asked to bear and to offer – their share in the Cross – it's not the same at all as the kind that comes from feeling our disharmony with God. How much of it comes to each of us and for how long, is His affair, not ours – but we must accept it with gratitude and use it as well as we can. I agree that it is very likely that you will be given a good deal of it; and anyhow the radiant, consoled prayer of God's vivid Presence is rather a beginner's prayer really and sooner or later – when God sees you are strong enough – He is certain to use your power of prayer for His redemptive purposes and that is always painful. No one – not the greatest saint – goes on in that lovely light all the time. You will have just common grey weather and storm and fog and perhaps even intense darkness before you have done – that's all part of the 'Leave all and follow Me.' But it's all right. I would not forecast anything or try to look ahead or wonder how much you can bear – just leave yourself in God's Hand. 'I am with thee, saith the Lord.' If you feel a definite pressure to leave contemplative prayer, and pray for others – then you must obey each time. But where it is left to you, give a little time anyhow to acts of simple love towards God. It soothes and braces us to remember His Beauty and be glad of it even when we don't see it at all. I think that's all for the moment – except of course avoiding strain, getting enough fun and so forth.

To L.K., 6 November 1934, *Letters*, pp. 238–9

# Abandonment to God

I am afraid you are going through a very bad bit of readjustment just now – that feeling one is of no use any more, is horrible but *is* a temptation of the devil . . . In various degrees I am sure we all have to make that transition. You and I have both been allowed a good run of active work, but the real test is giving it up, and passively accepting God's action and work, and the suffering that usually goes with it. It will mean not only interior growth for you, but also in the end, a closer union with God and greatly increased power of helping souls . . .

No one, not even the greatest saint, is irreplaceable. It is a greater act of trust and love to give your work into fresh hands than to struggle on with increasing damage to health. I know it must be increasing anguish to you – but after all, Our Lord Himself had to leave His work to twelve quite inferior disciples. We have to learn how to accept for ourselves all that this means, before we are really abandoned to God.

To Lucy Menzies, Trinity VI, 1938, *Letters*, p. 340

# THE CROSS

*Throughout these extracts the inseparability of the Cross from our lives and from our prayer has been stressed: in the simplest household duties, in the way we pray for others, in the Eucharist, even in the way Christ heals us. The saints and mystics are those who joyfully take up their Cross and follow – undoubtedly for more sacrifice and pain. The spiritual and mystical paths culminate in union with Christ on his Cross.*

*This may often seem too hard, too frightening, too much beyond us. There were times when Evelyn felt this too, yet her spiritual journey was a growth in the perception of her true vocation and her willingness to accept the Cross. 'Progress', she wrote in 1920, consists in 'learning more about the Cross'. In 1924, she wrote in her journal that*

> *... The only complete life of real joy is in following Jesus straight from the Eucharist to Gethsemane – at least in full intention and desire – unlimited and unselective self-giving – redemptive surrender.*

*She pursued this in her journal in July 1927:*

> *I see that the sacramental life is and must be one with the crucified life. It is associated with Our Lord's whole sacrifice and incomplete without a share in the Cross. Must regard all suffering sent by God as an opportunity of this.*

*That she repeatedly failed – or felt she did – was borne out in other journal entries: In June 1929 she wrote: 'Have been spoilt child. Now must genuinely grasp the Cross', and 'Have ceased to make progress because I have refused to make sacrifices'.*

*Evelyn points out that there is no joy in cowardice, and we are lacking in faith if we do not believe that Christ is within our limitations ensuring we are never alone. Like Julian of Norwich, Evelyn reminds us that Christ did not say we would not be given a rough time in this life, but that we would not be overcome. Our acceptance of this has far-reaching effects: 'We must accept the world's worst if we are to give it of our best.'[1]*

*Evelyn pursued the path of the Cross, and achieved a spirit of genuine serenity, peace and joy. Her words in this chapter provide us with encouragement: 'The first step taken towards Calvary was the worst: but in the first step all was achieved.'[2]*

*Are we prepared to take that step?*

1. Evelyn Underhill, *The School of Charity*, p. 59.
2. Evelyn Underhill, *The Fruits of the Spirit*, p. 29.

# The Strait Way to Calvary

The Light of the World enters our life to show us reality; and forces us to accept the fact that it is the whole of that life, not some supposed spiritual part of it, which is involved in our response to God, and must be self-given to the mysterious purposes of Charity. Christianity is a religion which concerns us as we are here and now, creatures of body and soul. We do not 'follow the footsteps of His most holy life' by the exercise of a trained religious imagination; but by treading the firm rough earth, up hill and down dale, on the mountain, by the lake-side, in garden, temple, street, or up the strait way to Calvary. The whole physical scene counts and is of vital importance to Christians; it can and does test us, save us or break us. So, to dismiss the pressures, limitations and crucial problems of practical life, bodily sufferings and self-denials, or even the most childlike and crude devotional exercises, as merely material, merely external, and so on, witnesses to a cheap and fundamentally unchristian attitude of mind; a complete misunderstanding of our real situation and the many-levelled richness of God's revelation within life. 'Dear Wood, dear Iron!' says the great hymn of the Cross, with relentless realism, 'Dear the Weight that hung on thee!'

*The School of Charity*, pp. 52–3

# Unconditional Self-Giving

It has been said that the whole of Christ's life was a Cross. I think that saying does grave injustice to its richness of response; the real joy and beauty of His contacts with nature, children, friends, the true happiness we find in the saints nearest to Him, the hours snatched for the deeply satisfying prayer of communion, the outburst of rejoicing when He discerns the Father's will. The span of perfect manhood surely includes and ratifies all this. But it was the deep happiness of the entirely self-abandoned, giving without stint truth, health and rescue, and always at His own cost: not the easy, shallow satisfaction of those who live to express themselves. There is a marked contrast between the first phase of the Ministry, with its confident movement within the natural world – healing what is wrong in it, and using what is right in it, and sharing with simplicity the social life of men and women – and the second phase, from the Transfiguration to the end. Then, we get a sense of increasing conflict with that same world, and the growing conviction that what is so deeply wrong with it can only be mended by a love that is expressed in sacrifice. The Suffering Servant, bearing its griefs and carrying its sorrows, is the one who most perfectly conveys the Divine Charity, and serves his brethren best.

'If anyone would come after Me, let him take up the Cross.' The spiritually natural life is very charming and the exclusively spiritual life is very attractive. But both stop short of that unconditioned self-giving, that willing entrance into the world's sufferings and confusion which God asks of rescuing souls. It was in the Passion, says St John of the Cross, that Christ 'accomplished that supreme work which His whole life, its miracles and works of power, had not accomplished – the union and reconciliation of human nature with the life of God.' Here we learn what it really means to volunteer for the Christian life.

*The School of Charity*, pp. 55–6

# The Source of Spiritual Growth

Quite early in the life of prayer we often begin feeling an exultant delight in God; religion seems full of love, joy and peace. And then that same spirit of love begins the relentless penetrating and transforming of our ordinary life; and things are not quite so nice. Life asks many distasteful tasks from us, shows us many inconvenient opportunities of love; asks long-suffering and gentleness and faithful perseverance, purifying us from all spiritual ambition and coming all the way down from the unlimited splendours of Divine Love to our very limited capacity, teaching us meekness and temperance. Just as at Pentecost the Infinite, Divine Charity came down on a group of very ordinary people and made them not spectacular saints but useful missionaries who kept all their human characters.

That is the path of the Spirit, transfiguring the souls it seeks. We might even dare to say that our Lord's life is, in some respects, a demonstration of this law. The joy and expansion of His communion with the Father and knowledge of His powers, culminating in the Transfiguration; the gentleness and long-suffering of the Ministry of Healing; the faithfulness that set His face towards the dangers of Jerusalem. And then the meekness, helplessness, utter humiliation of the Cross – and the self-control, the temperance which held His power in check, never forcing an issue, never using it for His own ends, accepting in full our creaturely status and thus gathering all into communion with God. When our Lord cried on the Cross, 'It is accomplished!' He had come down to the very bottom of the stairs and was self-identified through the Spirit of Love with the lowest, most despised and most despairing, and so He became the Source of the spiritual growth of all men and women.

*The Fruits of the Spirit*, pp. 9–10

# Forgiveness and Redeeming Love

Every soul that appeals for God's forgiveness is required to move over to His side, and share the compassionate understanding, the unmeasured pity, with which He looks on human frailty and sin. So difficult is this to the proud and assertive creature, that it comes very near the end of our education in prayer. Indeed, the Christian doctrine of forgiveness is so drastic and so difficult, where there is a real and deep injury to forgive, that only those living in the Spirit, in union with the Cross, can dare to base their claim on it. It means not only asking to be admitted to the Kingdom of Redeeming Love, but also declaring our willingness to behave as citizens of that Kingdom even under the most difficult conditions; the patriot king forgiving the invaders of his country, the merciful knight forgiving his brother's murderer and sheathing his sword before the crucifix, the parent forgiving his daughter's betrayer, the devoted reformer forgiving those who have ruined his life's work, the lover of peace forgiving the maker of war. Cruelty, malice, deceit and violence doing their worst; and seen by us through the eyes of a pitiful God. All this is supernatural, and reminds us again that the Lord's Prayer is a supernatural prayer; the prayer of the re-born, the realistic Christian who exists to do God's Will. Even so this clause comes a long way down: after the life of worship, the life of consecration, the prayer that the soul may be fed by the hand of God. Only then is it ready for this supreme test; this quiet and genial acceptance of the wounds of life, all the deliberate injury and the casual damage that come from lack of love; this prayer from the Cross. 'Love your enemies and pray for them that persecute you.' 'The Saints,' says St Teresa, 'rejoiced at injuries and persecutions, because in forgiving them they had something to offer God.'

*Abba*, pp. 65–6

# The Vocation of Sacrifice

Human beings are saved by a Love which enters and shares their actual struggle, darkness and bewilderment, their subjection to earthly conditions. By a supreme exercise of humility the deep purposes of God are worked out through our natural life with all its powers, humiliations, conflicts and sufferings, its immense capacity for heroic self-giving, disinterested love; not by means of ideas, insights, and spiritual experiences even of the loftiest kind. Charity, generosity, accepting the vocation of sacrifice, girding itself with lowliness as one that serveth and then going straight through with it, suffering long, never flinching, never seeking its own, discloses its sacred powers to us within the arena of our homely everyday existence: and it is by the varied experiences and opportunities of that daily existence, that our dull and stubborn nature shall be trained for the glorious liberty of eternal life.

The Word, the Thought of God, made flesh and dwelling among us, accepted our conditions, did not impose His. He took the journey we have to take, with the burden we have to carry. We cannot then take refuge in our unfortunate heredity, temperament, or health when faced by the demands of the spiritual life. It is as complete human beings, taught and led by a complete Humanity, that we respond to the pressure of God.

Grace does not work *in vacuo*: it works on the whole person, that many-levelled creature; and shows its perfect work in One who is described as Very Man, and of whom we cannot think without the conflict of Gethsemane and the surrender of the Cross.

There must always be something in this life which is the equivalent of the Passion and the Cross. Suffering has its place within the Divine purpose, and is transfigured by the touch of God. A desperate crisis, the demand for a total self-giving, a willingness to risk everything, an apparent failure, darkness and death – all these are likely to be incidents of a spiritual course. Those who complain that they make no progress in the life of prayer because they 'cannot meditate' should examine, not their capacity for meditation, but their capacity for suffering and love.

*The School of Charity*, pp. 53–4

# Partakers of Christ

'We are made partakers of Christ,' says the writer of *Hebrews*, 'if we hold the beginning of our confidence steadfast to the end.' The beginning is easy and lovely. It is the end that tests to the utmost our courage and love. 'Can you drink of My cup and be baptized with My baptism?' Not unless you care far more about God and His purposes than you do about your own soul; but that is the very essence of a spiritual life. Profound submission to the Will of God declared through circumstances: being what we are, and the word what it is, that means sooner or later Gethsemane, and the Cross, and the darkness of the Cross. Most of the saints have been through that. We do not begin to understand the strange power of the Passion, the light it casts on existence, till we see what it was in their lives.

For union with the Cross means experience of the dread fact of human nature, that only those who are willing to accept suffering up to the limit are capable of giving love up to the limit; and that this is the only kind of love which can be used for the purposes of the redeeming life. It is on Good Friday, and only then, that the ancient liturgies hail Christ as the Strong, the Holy, the Immortal; as if this crisis alone could disclose in its fullness His mysterious power. And it is at the Institution of the Eucharist, on the eve of that apparent failure, that they place in His mouth the words of the Psalmist, 'The right hand of the Lord bringeth mighty things to pass! I shall not die but live, and declare the works of the Lord!' Every Christian altar witnesses to that. The living power of Christ within the world, the Food He gives eternally to all, have been won by the costly exercise of a heroic love.

*The Mystery of Sacrifice*, pp. 57–8

# Praying from the Cross

The crowds who followed Christ hoping for healing or counsel did not ask Him to teach them how to pray; nor did He give this prayer to them. It is not for those who want religion to be helpful, who seek after signs; those who expect it to solve their political problems and cure their diseases, but are not prepared to share its cost. He gave it to those whom He was going to incorporate into His rescuing system, use in His ministry; the children of the Kingdom, self-given to the creative purposes of God. '*Thou* when thou prayest . . . pray ye on this manner.' It is the prayer of those 'sent forth' to declare the Kingdom, whom the world will hate, whose unpopularity with man will be in proportion to their loyalty to God; the apostles of the Perfect in whom, if they are true to their vocation, the Spirit of the Father will speak. The disciples sent out to do Christ's work were to depend on prayer, an unbroken communion with the Eternal; and this is the sort of prayer on which they were to depend. We therefore, when we dare to use it, offer ourselves by implication as their fellow workers for the Kingdom; for it supposes and requires an unconditional and filial devotion to the interests of God. Those who use the prayer must pray from the Cross.

*Abba*, p. 10

# Faithfulness: The First Step

Surely we may say that the chief struggle of the Passion, the awful crisis of Gethsemane, was a struggle in which we are shown the supreme heights of faithfulness, a struggle for strength to see it through to the end, whatever the cost. 'Let this cup depart . . . nevertheless not my will but Thine be done!'

The first step taken towards Calvary was the worst: but in the first step all was achieved. 'Be thou faithful unto death, and I will give thee the Crown of Life.' Faithfulness is one of the sturdy qualities most dear to the heart of God. Peter was offered just the same chance of the same royal virtue. Jesus was victorious on the Cross. Peter was defeated, warming himself by the fire for the night was cold. I wonder how *we* should act if the same sort of crisis, charged with fear and quite devoid of consolation, came our way? It is a crisis which in some form all the saints have had to face.

*The Fruits of the Spirit*, p. 29

# The World's Worst – God's Victory!

If then we look at the Crucifix and then at our selves, testing by the Cross the quality of our courage and love; if we do this honestly and unflinchingly, this will be in itself a complete self-examination, judgment, purgatory. It is useless to talk in a large vague way about the Love of God. Here is its point of insertion in our world, in action, example and demand. Every Christian is required to be an instrument of God's rescuing action; and His power will not be exerted through us except at considerable cost to ourselves. Muzzy, safety-first Christianity is useless here. We must accept the world's worst if we are to give it of our best. The stinging lash of humiliation and disillusionment, those unfortunate events which strip us of the seamless robe of convention and reserve, and expose us naked to the world in the weakness of our common humanity, the wounds given by those we love best, the revelation that some-one we had trusted could not be trusted any more, and the peculiar loneliness and darkness inseparable from some phases of the spiritual life, when it looks as though we were forsaken and our ultimate hope betrayed: all these are sufficiently common experiences, and all can be united to the Cross. Here again Christ remains within our limitations. He hallows real life, and invites us to hallow it by the willing consecration of our small humiliations, sacrifices and pains.

And indeed, unless we can do this our world is chaos; for we cannot escape suffering, and we never understand it till we have embraced it, turned it into sacrifice, and given ourselves in it to God. Then, looking from this vantage-point upon the Crucifix, we see beyond the torment and the darkness, the cruel physical pain and its results. As in some of the great creations of mediaeval art, we are allowed to discern the peace of a divine and absolute acceptance, a selfless and abandoned love, tranquil, unstrained, strangely full of joy: the joy of suffering accepted and transfigured by the passion of redeeming charity. And in the end, of course, we too only triumph by that which we can endure and renounce. The only victories worth having in any department of life must be won on Calvary.

*The School of Charity*, pp. 59–60

# Prayer in Darkness

We are never alone. We often feel that we make a mess of our suffering and lose the essence of sacrifice, waste our opportunity, fail God, because we cannot stand up to it. Gethsemane is the answer of the Divine Compassion to that fear.

We sometimes think we need a 'quiet time' before making a great spiritual effort. Our Lord's quiet time was Gethsemane; and we know what that was like.

We must, when the moment comes for us, endure in apparent loneliness the assault of sin, agony, and darkness. We too must elect for the Will of God when it means the complete frustration of our own efforts, the apparent death of our very selfhood; and only so enter into the life-giving life. We cannot expect to reflect the joy and the power of that strange victory, if we dodge the pain and conflict in which it was won. Prayer in darkness and forsakenness, the complete disappearance of everything that could minister to spiritual self-love, humiliating falls and bitter deprivations, the apparent failure even of faith, buffetings of Satan renewed when least expected, long sojourn in that solitary valley where Christian 'was so confounded that he did not know his own voice': these are all part of that long process, which sometimes seems like a plodding journey and sometimes like a swaying battle, through which the mighty purposes of the Divine Charity are fulfilled in human souls.

All this, the Creed assures us, is part of the inner life. Little wonder that the Christian must be sturdy about it; fit for all weathers, and indifferent to his interior ups and downs. Umbrellas, mackintoshes and digestive tabloids are not issued to genuine travellers on this way. Comfort and safety-first must give place to courage and love, if we are to become – as we should be – the travelling agents of the Divine Charity.

*The School of Charity*, pp. 61–2

# EPILOGUE

*In 1923, in an entry in one of her unpublished journals, Evelyn Underhill wrote:*

> *More and more I realize, the union with Christ one craves for can and must be only through union with His redemptive work always going on in the world. If I ever hesitate before this, and the pain and stress it must mean for us wretched little creatures used as his instruments – then I draw back from Him and break the link. So this 'life of supremely happy men (and women)' is not 'alone with the Alone' – it's the redeeming life, now and in Eternity too, in ever greater and more entrancing union with the Spirit of Jesus ceaselessly at work in the world.*

*This statement and the preceding extracts should surely dispel the notion that Evelyn Underhill presented a view of the spiritual life that was 'comfortable and private'. Her own spiritual journey was so often a 'Dark Night' experience: frightening, arduous, and intensely lonely. Yet her inner sufferings were well concealed from even her closest friends, who saw her always as joyful and good-humoured, patient and kind. She gave herself unstintingly to others then – and she gives of herself and her wisdom now.*

*In her day, Evelyn criticized the Church for being 'very busy pleasing men' – and presumably women too. Evelyn was not in the business of pleasing anyone but God – and so she did please. She pleased the right people, those with the right perspective and priorities.*

*The courageous stand she took, with a spirituality that could never circumvent the Cross and suffering, and her uncompromising, Gospel-oriented view of pacifism that expressed what the Church should have been professing and did not, proved that she could be 'in touch with the social and political realities of her time', and risk her reputation by embracing the unpopular minority stand if she believed it right. She did not condemn anyone else for not doing likewise. 'Only a very small number are ready for the Cross', she wrote, 'in the full sense of loving and unresisting abandonment to the world that may come.'[1]*

*Thus, the people to whom Evelyn Underhill appealed – those whom she 'pleased' – were those who were genuinely committed to taking up their Cross, and following Christ. They were not looking for what they could get out of religion, but were seeking to give – generously, heroically, completely.*

*Like Evelyn, they strove to be – given to God.*

1. Charles Williams (ed.), *The Letters of Evelyn Underhill*, p. 308.

# SOURCES

Armstrong, Christopher. *Evelyn Underhill*, Mowbrays, London and Oxford, 1975.

Brame, Grace. *The Ways of the Spirit*, Crossroad, New York, 1990.

Cropper, Margaret. *Evelyn Underhill*, Longman, London, 1958.

Egan, Harvey. *What Are They Saying About Mysticism?*, Paulist Press, Mahwah, New Jersey, 1982

Greene, Dana. *Modern Guide to the Ancient Quest for the Holy*, State University of New York Press, 1990.

Hartill, Percy (ed). *Into the Way of Peace*, James Clark, London 1940.

Kelsey, Morton, *The Other Side of Silence*, SPCK, London, 1976.

Underhill, Arthur, *Change and Decay*, Butterworth & Co, London, 1938.

Underhill, Evelyn. *Abba*, Longmans, Green & Co, London, 1940.

Underhill, Evelyn. *The Church and War*, Anglican Pacifist Fellowship, London, 1940.

Underhill, Evelyn, *Collected Papers*, Longmans, Green & Co, London, © 1946, Evelyn Underhill Estate.

Underhill, Evelyn. *Concerning the Inner Life*, Methuen & Co Ltd, London, 1926.

Underhill, Evelyn. *The Fruits of the Spirit*, Longmans, Green & Co, London, 1942.

Underhill, Evelyn. *The House of the Soul*, Methuen & Co Ltd, London, 1929.

Underhill, Evelyn. *The Life of the Spirit and the Life of Today*, Methuen & Co Ltd, London 1928.

Underhill, Evelyn. *Light of Christ*, Longmans, Green & Co, London, © 1944, Evelyn Underhill Estate.

Underhill, Evelyn. *Man and the Supernatural*, Methuen & Co Ltd, London, 1927.

Underhill, Evelyn. *A Meditation on Peace*, Fellowship of Reconciliation, London, 1939.

Underhill, Evelyn. *Mixed Pasture*, Methuen & Co Ltd, London, 1933.

Underhill, Evelyn. *The Mount of Purification*, Longmans, Green & Co, London, © 1949, Evelyn Underhill Estate.

Underhill, Evelyn. *The Mystery of Sacrifice*, Longmans, Green & Co, London, 1938.

Underhill, Evelyn. *Mysticism*, Methuen, London, 1911.

Underhill, Evelyn. *Mystics of the Church*, J Clarke, Cambridge, 1925.

Underhill, Evelyn. *Practical Mysticism*, J M Dent, London, 1914. (Current edition: Eagle, London, 1991).

Underhill, Evelyn. *The School of Charity*, Longmans, Green & Co., London, 1934.

Underhill, Evelyn. *The Spiritual Life*, Hodder and Stoughton, London, 1937. (Current edition: Mowbray, Oxford, 1984).

Underhill, Evelyn. *Worship* Nisbet, London, 1936. (Current edition: Eagle, London, 1991).

Williams, Charles (ed). *The Letters of Evelyn Underhill*, Longmans, Green & Co, London, 1943. (Current edition: Darton, Longman & Todd, 1991).